A Concise History of the Hawaiian Islands

A
Concise History
of the
Hawaiian Islands

Dr. Phil Barnes

Dedication

This book is dedicated to Hawai'i's residents of all races
who are working together to expand the spirit of aloha
into the dawn of the new millenium.

ISBN 0-912180-56-0

Published in Hawai'i by the Petroglyph Press, Ltd.
160 Kamehameha Avenue - Hilo, Hawai'i 96720
Phone (808) 935-6006 - Fax (808) 935-1553
BBInfo@BasicallyBooks.com
www.BasicallyBooks.com

Seven Printings
September 1999 ~ October 2003
Eighth Printing - August 2004

PREFACE

My goal in writing this book was to create a short book that travelers to Hawai'i can read in a few hours. One's travels become more meaningful when viewed within the context of a historical framework. Many archeological remains of prehistoric times can still be observed on all of the islands. Rich collections of early artifacts are not only found in museums but hotel lobbies. The Hawaiian Renaissance is much more than a marketing strategy for attracting visitors. Real change is in the air in the islands. This should be viewed as an exciting expansion of the aloha spirit rather than a threat to the status quo. May your appreciation of the cultural and environmental kaleidoscope of these beautiful islands be expanded by spending a bit of time in digesting this book. I have included a suggested reading materials list should you wish to expand your knowledge base.

I would like to thank my wife, Diane, for her support. I would also like to thank my daughter, Dr. Brooke Barnes, for extensive editorial assistance. Bob Voris and Dr. Beth Hartley are also thanked for their reviews of early drafts. Most of all I would like to thank the Hawaiian people for their perseverance against exceptional odds to keep the feeling of aloha alive in these islands that I love.

P. Kimo Barnes

Contents

Prologue

The Hawaiian Archipelago is one of the most remote groups of islands on the face of the planet. The Islands are over 2,400 miles from the closest continental land mass. This relative isolation has resulted in unique life forms and also accounts for the fact that the islands were one of the last spots on the globe to be populated.

The islands are all volcanic in origin with the youngest islands being on the southeast region of the chain. The islands are located on the Pacific plate. The plate moves slowly to the northwest. There is a hot spot that is stationary in the middle of the Pacific Ocean. This hot spot is actually a large vent where molten material flows to the surface. New islands are created in the southeast as the older islands slowly drift to the northwest. The island of Hawai'i, the newest island, is presently located over this hot spot. It emerged above the ocean surface less than one million years ago. It is the only island that still has active volcanoes. A new island, Lo'ihi, is forming to the southeast of the island of Hawai'i. It is still 3,000 feet underwater and will not break the surface for thousands of years.

Volcanic activity is still much in evidence on the island of Hawai'i. Of the five volcanoes that formed this island two, Kilauea and Mauna Loa, are still active. The east rift zone of Kilauea has been erupting almost continuously since 1983. Over 200 homes in this region as well as countless historical and ecologically unique areas have been covered over by this flow. You may still observe lava flowing into the ocean, creating massive clouds of steam at the end of Chain of Craters Road in Hawaii Volcanoes National Park.

Erosion and island sinking are constant forces at work here, as well as elsewhere on the planet. The oldest islands, such as French Frigate Shoals, are little more than coral heads a few feet above water at high tide, as the sea and other elements have been reducing their size since the moment when their volcanoes became dormant. These islands are uninhabited and are currently a refuge for nesting sea birds, sea turtles, and the

Hawaiian monk seals. They are under the jurisdiction of the U.S. Fish and Wildlife Service and all access other than scientific research is severely limited. At the other end of the chain are the mountains of the island of Hawai'i which rise almost 14,000 feet above sea level, with peaks often covered in snow. Erosive factors and sinking have not had time to make dramatic inroads in this young island. Dramatic illustrations of this erosive principal are the Na Pali coast on Kaua'i and the north shore of Moloka'i, which contains the highest sea cliffs on earth. Both of these sea cliffs or pali were created when massive chunks of the islands slid into the ocean during major earthquakes.

Of the 4,000 islands that compose the Hawaiian Archipelago there are eight major islands. These are in order from east to west: Hawai'i, Maui, Kaho'olawe, Lana'i, Moloka'i,

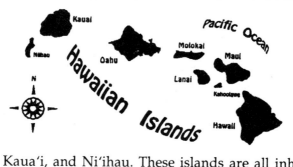

O'ahu, Kaua'i, and Ni'ihau. These islands are all inhabited except for Kaho'olawe which was used by the U.S. Navy for years as a bombing range. It has currently been returned to the Hawaiian people and it is being restored to its natural state. The size of these islands vary from Kaho'olawe to the island of Hawai'i which is almost twice as large as all of the other Hawaiian Islands combined.

Since the islands are so isolated, life forms were slow to develop and have evolved into a unique biota. All life forms arrived on the islands by means of one of the three w's. Wave action carried many life forms, particularly flowering plants, to the islands. Anyone who has seen a coconut sprouting on the shore can appreciate this form of plant dispersal. Wings is the second means of introduction. Obviously birds arrived in the region, both the pelagic sea birds who travel the earth's oceans and land based birds who made it to the islands in

6

powerful storm winds. Birds deposited many seeds in their feces as well as bringing insects and other life forms that were lodged in their feathers. Wind is the third natural pathway for the introduction of new species, particularly the high altitude jet stream that carries a heavy load of spores and other microscopic life forms.

Obviously these methods of dispersal would severely limit the gene pool in Hawai'i. With relatively few representatives from any given species and few total species, life forms evolved from a limited base to fill the many diverse ecological niches in the islands. Single species evolved into a great number of different but related species. The Hawaiian Honey Creeper, a small bird, is a good example of this phenomenon. Thirty separate species evolved from a single original species. Two-thirds of all species found on the islands when the first inhabitants arrived were endemic only to Hawai'i. The introduction rate of new species has increased dramatically since that time.

An unusual characteristic of the endemic fauna of Hawai'i is the fact that only two mammals were found on the islands before the first Polynesians arrived. These were the monk seal and a species of bat. This created an ecosystem with a distinct lack of predators. This is one of the reasons that introduced species have had such a devastating effect on the native species of plants and animals. A good example of this is the introduction of the mongoose in the 1930's. The goal was to find a predator to keep the rat population in check. As it turns out rats are nocturnal and mongooses are diurnal so they seldom come in contact. To make matters worse, mongooses eat even more of the native bird eggs than the rats they were brought in to control. Since that time the state has created an elaborate system to prevent the introduction of further new species.

There were also no native species of reptiles and amphibians. The large and varied insect population has given rise to an expanding number of predators in the form of lizards. Except for the earthworm size blind snake, there are still no snakes on the islands. This situation is presently being tested by the brown tree snakes from Guam. This poisonous snake has a propensity to stow away on airplanes flying into Hawai'i. Planes are inspected on landing to try to keep this new intruder from gaining a foothold in Hawai'i.

Chapter 1
First settlement

Before looking at the arrival of the first humans in Hawai'i, an examination of the voyaging traditions of the Polynesians is in order. Although there is still a scholarly debate on the origins and migration of the Polynesian peoples, the dominant theory is that they migrated from Asia to the Southeast Asian Peninsula and then continued across the sea into Indonesia. From there they followed an easterly route across Melanesia and Micronesia to the vicinity of Fiji. From this juncture one strand headed south to New Zealand. Another headed north, through the Society Islands, to the Marquesas and then on to Hawai'i. This should not be interpreted as a mass migration. It was more a series of fairly short voyages over perhaps a thousand years. As with the history of all groups before the advent of writing, it is possible to establish a chronological sequence from the oral histories, but exact dates can not be given. As a side note, Polynesia is described as the region included in a triangle with the western corner being New Zealand, the eastern corner Easter Island, and the northern point Hawai'i.

What drove these nomads of the seas? How and why did they shove off into uncharted oceans? The easy answer is that, like all peoples of the hunter-gatherer tradition, they were constantly searching for food, but it is not this simple. They had a history of agriculture and food harvesting technologies that allowed them to harvest the surplus of food that is essential for a people to create the rich civilization that characterizes this region. It is undoubtedly true that, even with this abundance of food, an area would eventually no longer be able to support the expanding population and a group would be formed to head out to sea in search of new lands. Tribal conflict could also be resolved by the less powerful group going their own way rather than engaging in warfare.

These expeditions were well planned so that the group would have all of the necessities that they required when they

Pua'a

reached their new home. They would carry livestock in the form of chickens, dogs, and pigs. They would also take select crops such as bananas, taro, and breadfruit to cultivate for future harvest. Medicinal plants would also be taken to ensure necessary remedies for healing rituals. Food for them and their animals would be required as well as water both for themselves and to water their plants. Basic tools, cordage, gourds, and other supplies would need to be included.

Perhaps more important than the physical materials that were taken would be the makeup of the crew themselves. There was commonly a crew of at least 15 people on each boat. Often three or four boats would travel together. This would provide an added element of safety at sea as well as a larger group of colonists to form their society on the new island when they landed. There would need to be a cross section of males and females as well as members of diverse families to avoid the problems associated with inbreeding. Individuals would also need to possess the skills to establish their new habitation, as well as those skills needed to pilot a craft in unknown waters for an extended voyage. And not all voyagers successfully completed their journey. No one knows how many of these pioneers perished at sea before being able to make a landfall.

Their methods of navigating are only recently being resurrected by Polynesians who wish to keep the voyaging traditions alive. This navigation was a combination of celestial observations such as marker stars at night and cloud formations during the day, as well as evaluating flotsam (objects floating in the water), bird and fish species that were sighted, current flow, etc. As the number of floating objects increased and they sighted birds with limited flight range they would know that they were getting closer to land days before an actual sighting would be made. This was a complex system that involved no instruments and, since writing was not present, had to be learned by rote memory.

The voyaging vessels themselves could take several different forms. They consisted of hulls that were created by hollowing out large logs. These dugouts were then decked with shaped wood pieces often made of Koa, a beautiful wood indigenous to the islands. The hollowed out area could then be used to store supplies in a dry environment. This hull would

Voyaging Canoe

either be joined to a similar hull to create a catamaran or have an outrigger attached to construct a stable and seaworthy craft. A platform was attached to the two hulls which created a living area for the voyagers. A small hut or shed roof was added for protection from the elements.

Vessels would be propelled by both sails and paddles. With the twin hull configuration ten or more people could be paddling at the same time. This was a distinct advantage over larger European style sailing ships in that they did not need to worry about becoming becalmed when the winds die for weeks on end in the tropical seas. These craft also had the advantage of drawing far less water than the larger sailing ships. It was thus much easier to navigate the dangerous coral shoals. The boats could be paddled directly onto the beach rather than mooring a quarter mile out to sea. This allowed them to escape the destructive force of the not uncommon tropical storms.

It is commonly speculated that the first Polynesians to reach Hawai'i came from the Marquesas Islands in what is now French Polynesia. These islands are some of the most inhospitable in all of the South Pacific. The main islands are ringed by sea cliffs and divided by valleys that are so deep that the bottom receives little direct sunlight. Thus access to both the bounty of the ocean and arable land for farming was extremely limited. The people had a reputation of being very warlike, which is common in areas with limited resources. All in all, it is not hard to imagine why a group would want to strike out for a more accommodating environment. The Marquesas are over 1,000 miles from Hawai'i. That would make this one of the longest voyages over open ocean in all of Polynesia.

Wherever their origin, the first landfall was made at Ka Lae on the southern coast of the island of Hawai'i. Again there is a debate as to the time of this arrival. Most estimates put this landing between 400 and 500 A.D. It is commonly speculated that the voyagers were probably running low on supplies when they reached Hawai'i. If they had missed Hawai'i, the next group of islands is the Aleutian Chain of Alaska, far to the north. If they were lucky, Mauna Loa may have been erupting at the time. At a height of 13,600 feet this beacon could be observed far out to sea, particularly at night. Even if the volcano was not erupting the great mass of the island's mountain creates its own weather system with clouds stacking up high into the sky. This would be a sign that the skillful navigators would not be likely to miss if they were even within 100 miles of the island.

Once a landfall was made they would quickly have gone to work to recreate the agricultural and domestic attributes of their homeland. They would of course be mindful of specific differences in their new surroundings and would modify their practices to adapt to the new environmental conditions. These original settlers had the islands to themselves for several centuries. During this time period they occupied all of the major islands in the Hawaiian chain. All of this was thrown into disarray around the year 1000 when a large contingent arrived from the islands of Tahiti. These new arrivals were physically larger and quickly established their dominance over the original inhabitants. In a relatively short period of time a new hierarchy was created, with the Tahitians as the ali'i or nobles and the former occupants reduced to the role of commoners.

Little is known of these smaller original inhabitants and some say they are the basis of the menehune mythology. These are the "little people" that come out only at night and are known for their engineering prowess. Many rock walls and other structures in the islands are attributed to their labor.

It is speculated that in the early years following the arrival of the Tahitians there was widespread voyaging between Hawai'i and Tahiti with a wholesale migration of large numbers of Tahitians and extensive trade between the two regions. For unknown reasons all contact with the rest of Polynesia suddenly ceased and the Hawaiian Islands remained isolated until the arrival of the Europeans almost 800 years later. It was during this time period that the rich culture of Hawai'i developed in a manner that allowed half a million inhabitants to exist in the islands with all of their physical needs being met with a minimum of difficulty. Their remaining free time could be devoted to all of those aspects of music, dance, and the arts that make Hawai'i such an interesting destination today.

Chapter 2
Pre-European Hawai'i

A complex system of government evolved in Hawai'i. Members of the ruling class were called ali'i. There was a broad variety of rank within the ali'i. High chiefs possessed absolute power comparable to kings in European culture. Kamehameha, in the early 1800's, was the first king to unite the entire island

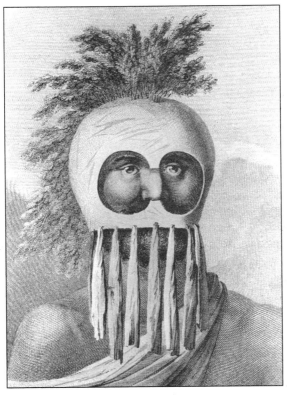

Warrior in a gourd helmet.

chain under one rule. Until that time there could be several ruling chiefs on the same island. This created a system of almost constant warfare, both between islands and within the larger islands. One of the first criteria for attaining status as an ali'i, besides heritage, was being a powerful warrior. It should be noted that the ali'i actually led their troops into battle in a literal fashion. In some battles the whole fight would be between the ranking ali'i on the two sides. When not involved in an actual conflict the men would be practicing military skills and waging mock battles. One of the most admired attributes of a warrior was the ability to catch a spear that was hurled at him in mid-air. Kamehameha was supposedly unsurpassed at this art.

One would think that all of this warfare would severely reduce the male population of the islands, but that was not the case. Most fighting was actually hand to hand combat. A battle could go on for days with few casualties. The object was to establish your superiority rather than to necessarily kill your opponent. This is related to the American Indian custom of counting coup, touching your enemy and escaping unharmed. Although many warriors were killed, the casualties could have been much higher.

As well as prowess in battle, ancestral rank was a critical factor in establishing status as an ali'i. This is why genealogy was extremely important in Hawaiian culture. It is not unusual to this day for Hawaiians to know their ancestors going back for 200 years. This made memory a highly valued trait before the era of written language. Children would play memory games from a very early age. An individual with an excellent memory could thus find a valued role in the community. They would commonly recite an ali'i's ancestry going back over 20 generations. Status could be further increased by marrying well. Unlike many cultures in which such behavior would be condemned, the highest level of status was achieved by marriage between siblings, if they were at the top rank. This practice of inbreeding could result in birth defects, and children born with visible defects would be killed at birth. Though this seems barbaric by today's standards, it was accepted as essential to maintaining a vigorous leadership.

The highest level of chiefs were called kapu moe. It was forbidden for commoners to even look at them or to let the ali'i's shadow fall upon them. These individuals would be at the top of their hierarchy, with lower ranking ali'i making up their court, like dukes and duchesses in the European system of monarchy. There was also a position like a prime minister. This individual was called the ali'i nui. Whether male or female this person wielded considerable power. The presence of the ali'i nui allowed for critical decision making even when chiefs were off at battle, or less commonly when chiefs were killed.

This Hawaiian aristocracy had all of the trappings of a royal class. The distinctive feather capes, which reached to the ground in the highest ranking individuals, were created from the bright red and yellow feathers of hundreds of thousands of birds, which were often released after the prized feathers were removed. The same feathers were used in their arching headdress. Feathers were also used to create the tall kahili which preceded the ali'i wherever they went. Commoners were thus warned of the approaching royalty, and could either prostrate themselves on the ground or vacate the area.

The economic system was similar to feudalism in other parts of the world. Ali'i held pie shaped sections of land called ahupua'a. Each unit would have a chief and minor ali'i. They would control a piece of land that extended from the ocean to the mist covered highlands. As they had at their disposal the variety of resources located at various elevations above sea level, they were relatively self sufficient and not highly dependent on trade. The ali'i did not actually own these plots of land, but were granted their use in return for loyalty to the king who owned all of the land. Within an ahupua'a individual families or ohana would occupy an ili, which was a narrow strip also running from the mountains to the coast.

Uhu

The oceans provided fish, shellfish, seaweed, salt and other necessities. The fish ponds were an interesting and unique use of coastal lands. This was one of the first examples of aquaculture on the planet. Rock walls were built to enclose a small bay. Sections of the wall had small holes that allowed water, small fish fry, and invertebrates to enter. As these fish fed on the marine life in the pond they would grow too large to swim back through the holes and would be trapped. They also used the pond to store their surplus harvest of fish. If they caught more fish than could be readily consumed they would place the excess living fish in the pond. The fish could then be easily netted from the enclosure when needed.

Not surprisingly most of the permanent settlements were located in this coastal region. Middle elevations were best suited for the farming of various kinds of fruit trees and crops. From the uplands they harvested the large trees, such as Koa, that were essential for some of their projects, such as the construction of voyaging canoes. The Sandalwood trees that played such a vital role in lucrative post-contact trade in the early 1800's were also found at these higher elevations.

An interesting aspect of this system was the role of the commoners, the maka'āinana. These individuals were in no form slaves or property of the ali'i. They were free to move about at their will, though they would often occupy the same land for generations. While they were occupying a particular parcel of land a portion of their harvest would be shared with the local noble. This would usually take place during the makahiki harvest season in the fall. They would also be available to pitch in to help with various construction projects, or other communal chores. As mentioned previously, the ali'i had absolute power. However, if they exercised this power in a ruthless or cruel fashion they risked alienating their subjects, who were free to take their allegiance elsewhere. This would force the ali'i into a certain degree of restraint. Ali'i who abused their subjects routinely would never rise to higher levels as they would be lacking a sufficient number of followers.

Each group of ali'i would also have their kāhuna. Although the title of kahuna is defined as a highly skilled master in one of many disciplines, it is used here to describe religious leaders. These priests were consulted by the leaders before any important decisions were made. Questions such as when to fish, go into battle, plant crops, etc. would need to be answered by the kāhuna before these projects were undertaken. Though they served as trusted advisors, they did not question the authority of the ali'i. The kāhuna carried on very long and complex ceremonies seeking a favorable intervention of the gods. Many of these ceremonies involved recitations of over an hour. In some instances the kahuna could be killed if a mistake was made in the ceremony. This insured a long and complex apprentice period before an individual could rise to this highly valued role.

The major gods of the Hawaiian's religion played an important role in the rich and diverse mythology of Hawai'i. Lengthy volumes have been devoted to this topic. This will be an overview of the four major gods. Kane is considered the major god, and creation stories are often centered around him. Lono is the god whose intercession is sought for fertile soils and a rich harvest. Ku is the god of war and was the chief god of Kamehameha. The last of the four, Kanaloa is considered the god of the sea. These gods are different from traditional gods in that they take on various characteristics in their different forms. For example, Kanehekili is lightning. Kumokuhali'i is the god of the upland forest, where the large trees needed to construct the ocean-going canoes are found. He was therefore venerated by canoe builders.

Pele Rising

There are a large number of minor gods. The most famous of these is Pele, the goddess of volcanoes. Inhabitants of the island of Hawai'i, her current home, still frequently make offerings to Pele. Her home in Halema'uma'u in Hawai'i Volcanoes National Park is a frequent stop for travelers to the island. It should be obvious that this was a nature-based religion. Hawaiians have always been very much in touch with the land or aina. Along with these universal gods, each family had their own ancestral spirits, called aumakua. They were often a fish, bird or other animal that had a particular significance to that family. The men of the family would make daily offerings to these spirits. Family members would make great efforts not to disturb their aumakua, whether it be a shark, sea cucumber, caterpillar, or other life form.

Heiau, or temples, were created to honor these gods. The size would vary from small platforms sometimes created from one rock, to elaborate structures that could take years to construct. These larger heiau were raised platforms created from large numbers of stones. They would be solid rather than just walls. It was not unusual for one to be 70 by 40 feet and 12 feet thick. Rocks were passed from great distances by people lined up in a long chain, in a bucket-brigade fashion. The top of these platforms often contained carved wooden representations of the gods, an offering tower, and a small hut where the leaders could gather. Heiau dedicated to Ku, the war god, would require periodic human sacrifices. The offering of a high ranking ali'i would be considered the most powerful. The individual was not always killed at the temple. He might have already been killed in battle and was then brought to the heiau as an offering. There are a large number of heiau that are still standing. It is not unusual to see fresh offerings of flowers or fruit located in their towers.

A discussion of Hawaiian religion is not complete without a look at the kapu system. A kapu, or taboo, is a thing or behavior which is forbidden, or a person, place or thing which is set apart as sacred or cursed. One example is those things that were universally forbidden, like women eating with men, or commoners interacting with high ali'i. Another form was when a specific action was outlawed for a set period of time. An example of this type of kapu would be when fishermen were forbidden to fish for a specific species of fish for a month. When Captain George Vancouver gave Kamehameha some cattle, a kapu was placed on them for over twenty years. The Ali'i's favorite surfing breaks could be kapu to commoners, as would the best canoe launch sites. Kāpu were therefore the major means that the ali'i used to maintain control over the commoners.

The breaking of a kapu could often result in death. There was an interesting Hawaiian system for gaining a reprieve if a kapu was broken. If the offender could escape and make it to a place of refuge, or pu'uhonua, he could be granted a pardon by the kāhuna and return home with no fear. However, making it to one of these locations was anything but easy. Often the main access was from the ocean and there were dangerous reefs that made getting ashore a tricky proposition. Land access would be obstructed by a well guarded, tall rock wall. People could also gain safety in time of war in these secure havens. An excellent example of a place of refuge can be found today south of Kealākekua Bay on the Kona coast of the island of Hawai'i. Pu'uhonua o Honauanau National Historical Park is being restored to its original condition of the late 1700's.

The Hawaiian family system is the essential element of the social structure of the islands. The main configuration was an extended family, the ohana. As mentioned previously, these ohana would occupy a slice of the ahupua'a and would have houses in the highland rain forest, mid-elevation farmlands, and on the coast. Certain family members would live at a particular elevation and participate in whatever subsistence activities were located at that level, such as raising taro and bananas at a mid-elevation homestead. They would give their surplus produce to other ohana members. Coastal members would give surplus fish and seaweed to upper elevation family members. This was not really a barter system but more just sharing your bounty with the rest of your relatives.

Family members tended to spend more time at the coast for many reasons, so the largest house would be built near the ocean. Any members of the ohana, as well as guests, could sleep there. One half of this house was a raised sleeping platform. It was covered with a thick layer of mats for sleeping comfort. There was a well defined pattern of who slept next to whom. Wives would sleep next to their husbands. Children slept in the same area, but there was no roughhousing allowed. They had to go outside if they wanted to play.

Unlike contemporary housing customs, there were a large

number of different structures, each with a specific function. Most were communal and could be used by all members of the ohana. The largest structure in a settlement would be the hale noa described above. Women of the family had a house called the hale pea where they would stay while they were menstruating. Men were not allowed to enter the area under penalty of death. Men had their own house, called the moa, where women were not allowed. Men would eat in this structure as well as make the daily offerings to the family aumakua. There were other buildings where specific work could be carried out, such as a canoe building shed for men and mat weaving and tapa making structures for women.

© 1996 VAREZ/CI

Pounding Poi

Most of the cooking was done outdoors by the men. The preferred method for a large volume of food was the buried imu oven. A bed of hot coals would be prepared in a shallow pit in advance. Food to be cooked was wrapped in banana leaves. There would be several bundles of items including both vegetable and animal products arranged on the coals. A wrapped whole hog was often cooked in this manner. The pit would then be filled over with soil and the contents left to cook for many hours. The many commercial luau as well as large Hawaiian family gatherings still cook in this manner. During rainy weather there was a small hut that would be used specifically for cooking.

In early Hawai'i, marriage customs were often quite informal. Sometimes commoners would not even have a ceremony. People were well aware who was married to whom. Usually the union was one man and one woman. But a man could have more than one wife and a woman could have more than one husband. The first marriage partner would typically have more status than subsequent partners. However, if a first wife did not produce a child and a second wife did, then the second wife would have superior rank. Sexual customs were definitely more relaxed than was the case in Western culture. Hawaiians were more monogamous than the stories of the first missionaries would lead you to believe, however. The situation mentioned earlier of a sister marrying her brother was far less common than speculated. It would only be undertaken by ali'i of the highest rank. These ali'i almost always had additional husbands or wives, so few of their children would be produced by their relationship with their sibling.

Hula Dancer

Dance, or hula, took on many forms in Hawai'i. Hula would be performed by both men and women. Some forms of hula were sacred while others were performed for entertainment of both the dancers and audience. Hula played an important role in passing down the oral history from one generation to the next. All hula movements represent a particular action or event and so by following the movements you can see a story told in a most beautiful fashion.

The early Hawaiians definitely had a fondness for sports. Many of these were water based activities such as swimming, surfing, and canoe racing. The swimming ability of these individuals was amazing. Both boys and girls would swim daily from an early age. They could commonly swim distances in excess of a mile. Since so much of their daily life centered around aquatic activities, skill in the water was more of a necessity than a luxury. It is not unusual today to see a group of Hawaiians swim out one-half mile, spear fish for several hours and then return with a nice catch that they speared from depths of up to 100 feet without the use of scuba gear. The breathtaking agility of Hawaiian surfers is well known. The ability to ride the waves is even more impressive when you see the crude wooden boards that were used for hundreds of years before the invention of fiberglass. Skill with canoes in heavy surf was an essential survival skill as well as a sport to these maritime people. The official state sport in Hawai'i today is outrigger canoe racing, so the tradition continues.

© 1996
VAREZ/CI

Makahiki Competition

Many of the land based sports were related to skills needed in battle, such as wrestling and spear throwing. Sports were designed to test both the athlete's skill and strength. Moving large boulders is an example of the latter ability.

The major sporting time of the year was the fall harvest festival, the makahiki, in honor of the god Lono. During this three month festival there would be a cessation of all warfare. Rival ohana and ali'i rooted for their favorite athletes in a broad spectrum of both land based and aquatic sports. The winners of these competitions were local heroes and were accorded the status of valiant warriors. It was during a makahiki that Captain Cook, to whom we shall now turn, arrived in Hawai'i.

Chapter 3
Cook to Kamehameha

Captain James Cook was one of the most famous navigators ever to sail under the Union Jack. He had been exploring
in the South Pacific for many years before he ever saw Hawai'i.

Cook with a gathering of Hawaiians

He had a far better knowledge of Polynesian culture and customs than any European of his time. Generally he was considered to be more humane and respectful of indigenous cultures
than other explorers in the late 1700's. He was no doubt pater-
nalistic by modern standards, but this was the era of going
out to civilize the "savages". Cook made three voyages to the
South Pacific. It is his third voyage with which we are concerned. He had already visited the islands of central Polynesia,
including Tahiti. In late 1777 he headed north to once again
pursue that European dream of a northwest passage between
the Atlantic and Pacific Oceans. Cook was surprised when he
came upon a group of islands in the mid-Pacific. He sighted
the island of Hawai'i first, but the northeasterly trade winds
pushed him too far to the west to make a landfall. The same
thing happened with succeeding islands until Cook finally

ended up at Kaua'i on the western end of the chain. Cook was seeking fresh water and provisions. With his knowledge of the Tahitian language he had little difficulty communicating with the many Hawaiians who paddled out to meet the ship.

He received a warm welcome and began trading for the needed provisions. He made an earnest attempt to keep all of his sailors on board, since he was aware that many of them were infected with syphilis. He was not successful in this attempt and a new disease was released in the islands. He was surprised to find that the natives were mainly interested in trading for iron objects. Since these were uncharted islands he wondered how they were aware of the existence of iron. This has led to speculations that perhaps the British were not the first explorers to reach Hawai'i. The re-provisioning went on without problems until some of the Hawaiians were caught stealing iron objects. The rate of theft increased until Cook felt it necessary to leave. The two craft resumed their northerly direction in search of the northwest passage, but not before noting the location of the islands on their charts. Cook named the islands after his friend and benefactor, the Earl of Sandwich.

After a summer and fall of fruitlessly searching in Alaska for the "passage", Cook's two ships, the Resolution and the Discovery, headed south. It was at this point that a number of accidental occurrences caused Cook to arrive in Kealakekua Bay in a manner that resulted in the natives perceiving him to be the god, Lono. As Cook neared Hawai'i he planned to make landfall on Maui. Unfavorable winds lead him to cross the channel to the island of Hawai'i. In his search for a good moorage he circled the island in a clockwise direction, ending up at Kealakekua Bay on the south Kona coast. He fulfilled three of the predictions for the return of Lono that had been prophesied by the kāhuna. First he arrived during the makahiki festival in honor of Lono. Second he approached from the south. And third his large multi-sailed square-rigger looked like the cloud on which Lono was predicted to arrive.

Cook was undoubtedly surprised by his newfound status when he came ashore. In typical fashion, however, he put his position to good use and received many of his provisions for free, without the usual bartering. After months at sea the crew was more than willing to take full advantage of this situation.

Cook did not attempt to keep his men on board on this arrival as it would have led to certain mutiny. Many local women stayed on the ships and sailors took up quarters on shore. With this welcome, Cook even set up an astronomical observatory on shore to gather data on the constellations. His artist, John Webber, filled sketch books that were later published to illustrate Cook's journals. Unfortunately, the British overstayed their welcome. After almost six weeks at the bay they had seriously depleted the resources of the region, and stealing was again becoming a major problem.

Cook then sailed north for Maui. A storm came up in the Maui Channel, which is common, and the Resolution was demasted. With no options, Cook limped back to Kealakekua Bay for the necessary repairs. The Hawaiians were not happy about this turn of events and theft became a major problem from the outset. The situation was so tense that Cook fired his main cannons as a show of force. The scene became desperate when a group of natives stole a skiff during the night. Cook was outraged and dispatched a shore party, including himself, to take the ruling ali'i, Kalaniopu'u, hostage to use as ransom for the return of the skiff. All went well at first and the chief came along without resistance. When his wife started screaming and pleaded with him not to go the chief refused to go with Cook. Things rapidly deteriorated, with the British being forced back to the shore. One of the sailors fired a musket loaded with shot at a native in reed armor. The gun misfired and the pellets bounced harmlessly off the vest. This gave the natives renewed confidence and they attacked with clubs swinging. Cook was killed by repeated blows to the head, and his body was taken. The rest of the British retreated to their ship. The Hawaiians believed that a person could gain the power of an enemy by taking possession of his body and some suspect that parts of Cook's body were eaten. After much dickering the British were able to gain possession of parts of Cook's body. No one knows what became of the rest. Later a monument was established by the British Navy at the site of Cook's death. They still return to the site and perform a ceremony in honor of the most famous explorer of the Pacific.

The British left with Captain Charles Clerke in command to return to England. Captain George Vancouver, a veteran of Cook's voyage, led several return expeditions to Hawai'i. The

British came to be well respected by the Hawaiians in succeeding years. This respect is demonstrated by the fact that the Union Jack is located in the upper left hand corner of the Hawaiian flag.

Now that Hawai'i was on the charts it became a major re-provisioning port for European and American merchants and whalers doing business in the Pacific. A few foreigners, or haoles, remained in the islands. Some became advisors to the ali'i in subsequent years. Others were idle beachcombers enjoying a carefree life.

One of the young Hawaiians who was present at Cook's death was a rising ali'i named Kamehameha, the nephew of Kalaniopu'u. In the aftermath of the European "discovery" he rose to power, becoming the first Hawaiian to rule as king of all of the islands. He was well versed in the arts of war and had the ability to see how to use the technology of the foreigners to his advantage.

On the eve of Kamahameha's birth it was prophesied that a male would be born who would overthrow the king. Like King Herod before him, the local king perceived the solution to be killing all male babies born at the time. Kamehameha's mother, who was a middle ranking ali'i, fled to the barren Kohala Coast of Hawai'i to give birth. The spot can be visited today above the powerful waves crashing to shore on the northernmost point of the island. Maui is visible across the channel on a clear day. His mother then hid the infant with relatives till he was six years old and the threat had passed. Kamehameha lived the life of an ali'i youth, spending countless hours in physical training as well as learning all of the protocols necessary to his position. It should be mentioned that Kamehameha was a massive man. From measurements taken of his cape, which still resides in the Bishop Museum in Honolulu, he was estimated to be almost seven feet tall and weighed over 300 pounds.

The main chief on the Island of Hawai'i at the time of Cook's visit, Kalaniopu'u, died in 1782. His choice for succession was unusual, and proved to be a recipe for conflict. He named his son, Kiwala'ō, as his successor, but placed his nephew, Kamehameha, in charge of war by bequeathing him the talisman of the war god, Kūkailimoko. Since war was essential to the maintenance of power this created an immediate problem for his son. Was his father purposefully testing him? This would seem the case as it was unlikely that the two would share power. Avoiding immediate aggression, Kamehameha withdrew from the Kona region and established himself at Kawaihae near his ancestral home in Kohala. Kiwala'ō eventually attacked first and many ali'i defected from Kamehameha. The winner of the conflict remained unclear however as Kiwala'ō was killed in battle.

Kamehameha the Great

It was shortly after this that Kamehameha came in contact with two young Englishmen, John Young and Isaac Davis. Rather than kill these captives he put them to work for him. They showed him how to most effectively use his captured guns and cannon. Kamehameha had small cannons mounted on his double hulled war canoes. John Young became one of his most trusted advisors over the years. Young married a Hawaiian woman and built a fine New England style home near Kamehameha's compound at Kawaihae.

A young American who gained favor with Kamehameha was John Parker. Captain George Vancouver had presented Kamehameha with several cattle in the early 1790's. The king placed a kapu on these cattle and let them run free to multiply in the uplands of the island. With no natural predators the wild cattle increased their numbers to the point where they were trampling crops and generally terrorizing villagers. Kamehameha hired the young Parker, who had jumped ship, to bring the cattle under control. Through resourcefulness the former sailor was able to capture some of the cattle and eventually to domesticate them. Many of the other cattle were butchered and a new meat was introduced to the Hawaiian diet. Parker was given a few acres as a reward and expanded his holdings considerably when he married one of Kamehameha's granddaughters. He brought over Mexican cowboys to train the Hawaiians, who would come to be called paniolos, in the arts of riding, roping, and other cowboy skills. He built his ranch into the dynasty that is today the largest privately owned ranch in the United States.

At this time Kamehameha's ambitions turned from the island of Hawai'i to Maui. Both Maui and O'ahu were controlled by the king, Kahekili. While he was away on O'ahu, Kamehameha attacked Maui. To avoid lengthy warfare the two signed a truce that both assumed would be temporary. Kamehameha returned to the island of Hawai'i to consolidate his power there. His chief rival on the island, Keoua, attacked shortly after his return from Maui. Kamehameha repulsed the invasion. While returning home via Mauna Loa there was an explosive volcanic eruption and Keoua lost one-half of his troops. Kamehameha and others took this as a sign that Madame Pele was opposed to Keoua, who was severely disheartened by the event.

Kamehameha next decided to build a large heiau to Ku, the god of war. This heiau, called Pu'ukoholā, is still standing in Kawaihae and is part of the National Park system. It is the site of numerous cultural and religious events by Hawaiians and other Polynesians. Kamehameha built this impressive structure by creating a human chain almost 20 miles long. Rocks were passed from hand to hand to the kāhuna who oversaw their placement. Kamehameha invited Keoua to the dedication of this heiau. Since the heiau required a human sacrifice, and the higher ranking the person the better, Keoua should have seen what was coming. He might have been so disheartened by his last defeat that he just placed his fate in the hands of the gods. In any case, his canoes were attacked before they even came ashore and he became the sacrifice that gave mana, or power, to the heiau. Kamehameha's control of the island of Hawai'i was never again in doubt. From this base he could pursue his dream of unifying the Hawaiian islands.

Kahekili, the king of Maui and O'ahu, then attacked Kamehameha. This was the first of a new style of warfare for Hawai'i. Both of the leaders possessed cannons and fought a major sea battle in the European style. After hours of shelling, the battle developed into a stalemate without a victor. Kamehameha's opportunity came when Kahekili died in 1794 and his sons fought one another for control of his territory. This played into Kamehameha's hands as he defeated his rivals one at a time. Perhaps the most famous battle of this campaign was the battle for control of O'ahu. Kamehameha forced his opponents up Nu'uanu Valley, in present day Honolulu, and backed them up to a 1,000 foot pali, or cliff, where many fell or leapt to their deaths rather than surrender.

At this point he controlled all of the Hawaiian Islands except Kaua'i. Kaua'i is over 70 miles from O'ahu. The Kaua'i Channel is by far the largest stretch of open water between any of the Hawaiian Islands. The Kaua'i Channel is known for violent storms that spring up without warning. This gave the island a relative degree of isolation from the warfare that occupied the other islands. It was only a matter of time until Kamehameha made his move, which came in 1804. He attacked with a large armada, but a storm sank many of his ships, forcing a hasty retreat to O'ahu. After another futile attempt at conquering Kaua'i he signed a treaty with the ruling chief, Kaumuali'i, making him the governor of the island. He agreed to pay an annual tribute to Kamehameha and thus the unification of the islands was completed.

The following years saw a period of peace developing in the islands. The monarchy was now solidified and the ali'i remained unified under Kamehameha's rule. He had wisely decided that from an administrative position it was effective to name a ranking ali'i to the position of governor of each of the major islands. One of his first appointments was to place a young ali'i named Boki as governor of O'ahu. Along with his wife, Liliha, he was to serve three successive monarchs in this capacity. Interactions with the Europeans and Americans increased dramatically during this period, but Kamehameha's force of personality was able to keep them well under control. He died at the age of 70 in 1819, on the eve of the most far reaching invasion of all.

Chapter 4
Missionaries & Whalers

It was the arrival of the Congregational missionaries in 1820 that set in place forces that were to ultimately reshape the future of Hawai'i. The period of foreign influence following Captain Cook's death had a profound effect upon future developments. The location of Hawai'i at the mid-point in the Pacific Ocean made it a natural site for re-provisioning ships of all countries wishing to become major players in the rapidly developing trade with Asia. British merchants were quick to see the possibilities of this new "discovery". They wasted no time convincing the ali'i to seek increased status in the owning and wearing of European clothing, furniture, and all manner of manufactured goods. Weapons of war such as cannon and muskets were in particular demand while the fight for domination of the islands continued. Kamehameha was proud of these new modern goods and the fad was enshrined.

The first trade commodity to allow the ali'i to make these purchases was sandalwood. This highly prized wood could be sold in China for enormous profit by European and American traders. This very slow growing tree was found in the upper elevations of the islands. The ali'i forced their subjects to harvest the wood and carry it down the slopes for loading. This work was so undesirable that the workers pulled up any seedlings of the tree that they found to hasten its extinction. The chiefs were now constantly in debt as they acquired more and more European goods. The bonanza could not last and these trees drew near to extinction in less than 20 years. The main role that Americans played in this trade was that they owned many of the ships that were hauling cargo between China and Europe. This shipping boom developed a market for ship re-provisioning by the Hawaiians. This, rather than sandalwood, had a lasting effect on the long term growth of the economy. Ships would always need fresh water, food, and a place for their sailors to get some rest and relaxation.

Against this backdrop of an expanding economy the American missionaries arrived just six months after the death of Kamehameha. Liholiho, Kamehameha II, was the new king, although in fact Kamehameha's favorite wife, Ka'ahumanu, was running things. It was largely due to her influence that the long standing kapu system came to an end. The event that broke the system was when she decided to eat with the men, one of the most strongly forbidden behaviors. The kāhuna were irate over this violation of tradition, but the ali'i stood behind her. When it was seen that the gods did not intervene and punish her, Hawaiians saw little reason to uphold the other kapu. In a very short time the traditional system that had maintained order in the islands for almost a thousand years had been abandoned by a large percentage of the populace. According to some accounts, Hawai'i was rapidly approaching anarchy when the missionaries arrived. Their timing could not have been better.

Ka'ahumanu

On their arrival the missionaries from New England quickly established bases on the islands of Maui, Hawai'i, and O'ahu. The lack of clothing worn by the women and the relatively lax sexual mores shocked the missionaries and they were not reticent about expressing these feelings. Many viewed the Hawaiians as savages to be saved from the fires of hell. Consequently it should come as no surprise that their welcome was less than enthusiastic. The missionaries steadfastly maintained their traditional manner of clothing and food preferences, although these were clearly unsuited to their new environment. This only served to further alienate them from the natives. This rigidity was diametrically opposed to the laid back life style of the islanders. The one bright spot in attracting the islander's interest was the fact that many had wanted to learn to read and write since their introduction to Western cultures. The ali'i were particularly eager students. Literacy would be a great advantage in their business dealings with the Anglos. The missionaries considered the ability to read the Bible an essential element of Christianity and were eager to teach these skills to the Hawaiians. Thus knowledge of Jesus was interspersed with basic language fundamentals. The first converts were ali'i who quickly applied pressure on their subjects to join the church. The beliefs filled a void left when the traditional religious beliefs declined. Converts were required to take formal exams to prove their knowledge of both English and Christianity before they would be accepted into the church. By 1830 fully 30% of Hawaiians were undergoing formal training to pass these exams.

While the missionaries were grateful to the ali'i for their patronage, they questioned the somewhat arbitrary power of the monarchy. As Americans, they also felt compelled to spread the concept of democracy to the islands. Rather than pushing for an outright change of the government, which would have surely failed, they had to settle for just planting the seeds and waiting for them to grow. The success of the missions did not go unnoticed. More recruits from the States were summoned and by 1838 the number of missionaries had increased to 90. They established Punahou School as a college prep institution for their children. In later years the youth of the wealthy sugar planters and businessmen attended as well. Punahou remains a distinguished school to this day and prides itself on the number of graduates who enroll in the Ivy League.

The monopoly of the Congregationalists did not go unchallenged for long. In 1831 a group of Catholic missionaries arrived from France. They were not only not welcomed, they were locked up under the pretense that they were French spies out to weaken British influence. The American missionaries played no small role in this subterfuge. The prisoners were not released until a French frigate aggressively sailed into Honolulu Harbor and fired a few rounds from its cannons. Undoubtedly the most famous Catholic priest in Hawai'i was the Belgian, Father Damien. He arrived at the leper colony on the Kalaupapa Peninsula on the island of Moloka'i in 1873. He ministered to the lepers for 16 years until he eventually died from the disease. He is currently being considered for saint-hood by the Catholic church.

Around the same time as the missionaries another very different group of Americans became interested in Hawai'i. These were the whalers that were home based in Massachu-setts. These ships started arriving in Lahaina and Honolulu in 1820. By 1824 there were 100 ships using Hawai'i as both a re-provisioning center, and a repository where they could off load their catch and continue whaling rather than return to New England whaling ports.

Another function of a stop in port was the opportunity to allow the sailors to blow off some steam after being confined to tight ship's quarters for months on end. It was this recre-ational aspect that put the whalers on a collision course with the missionaries. Stories of sailors fondness for rum are often not an exaggeration. The many grog shops lining the harbors of whaling ports were a true vexation to the tee-totaling cler-ics. They tried without success to get them closed down. The profits from the sale of alcohol caused many a believer to look the other way. A unique cottage industry also sprang up in Hawai'i at this time. When the drunken sailors were thrown in jail it would be necessary for a consul to intercede with the ali'i to secure their release. The best of these consuls suppos-edly made over $150,000 a year under the table. It was just a cost of putting into port in Hawai'i.

However, the sailors also created another, far more seri-ous, problem and that was the spread of sexually transmitted diseases to the island women. It was customary for young women to swim out to the ships entering port. They would exchange their favors (as they say) for clothing, perfume, cash or whatever else was available. In later periods these activities would be relegated to port side brothels as in most port towns. The missionaries pleaded with the ali'i to keep the women from swimming out to the ships, and after lengthy discussions the leaders agreed. This did not remove the temptation, however, as the women would meet the sailors in the bars and return with them to their ships. The ali'i then decided that the sailors could not spend the night in town and the women could not go to the ships. This edict was more than the seamen could tolerate and the skippers of several vessels protested the decision. In one of many disputes between Governor Boki and Ka'ahumanu he sided with the whalers. She remained steadfast, however, and the girls stayed on shore. When the whalers protestations proved unsuccessful a particularly incensed skipper, aptly named "Mad Jack" Percival, proclaimed that this was a declaration of war. He landed with a large number of sailors with the intention of burning down the church to teach the missionaries not to interfere in his affairs. His party was met by a large contingent of Hawaiians. As previously mentioned, many of the Hawaiians were very large men and there could be no doubt of the outcome. The missionaries had won this round, but the conflict was far from resolved.

Early Honolulu Harbor scene

The whaling industry benefitted the economy of the Islands in a number of ways. Many young Hawaiians were hired by the ships as crew. They usually worked out well, as nautical skills were an integral part of their Polynesian heritage. Extracting and refining whale oil created an industry of its own. Processing the whalebone, most famous as the framework of women's corsets, spun off as another business enterprise. But most of all the merchants who both bought the oil and provided the supplies needed by the whalers started to grow into powerful financial trading companies. Whales in the immediate vicinity of Hawai'i were quickly depleted and the whole process of whaling proved to be extremely cyclical. However, most of the whales processed in Hawai'i were caught in the frigid waters of the North Pacific and Arctic Oceans. One out of every five years would be an economic disaster. It was hard to make accurate predictions at all times. Still the industry managed to grow. At its height in the 1850's over 500 ships per year were making regular stops in the islands. The Hawaiians had 19 whaling ships of their own at the peak of the industry.

Whaling was not done in by over harvest, as many assume. The discovery of oil by Drake in Pennsylvania in the late 1850's, though barely noticed at the time, was the beginning of the gradual decline of the whaling industry and the end of American involvement in the industry. Kerosene lamps quickly reduced the demand for whale oil. One by one other whale-based products were replaced by cheaper synthetic substitutes.

Only the merchants and trading companies, who had begun to diversify years earlier, were able to remain financially viable after the crash of the whaling industry. They too might have gone under if it were not for the arrival of the industry that was to sustain Hawai'i for the next 100 years - sugar.

Chapter 5
Sugar Industry

Sugar cane was one of the crops that Hawaiians traditionally took with them when they set off for new lands. So the cultivation of sugar was nothing new to Hawai'i. The first large scale commercial sugar plantation was started in 1835 on the island of Kaua'i. This was a 1,000 acre plantation on land leased from the king. However, the cultivation of sugar cane underwent a dramatic transformation beginning in the 1850's. Ironically, the California gold rush of 1848 was one of the driving

Kamehameha III

factors for this new industry. It was quicker and cheaper to ship agricultural products, including sugar, from Hawai'i than the Eastern Seaboard of the U.S. at this time. The potential agricultural prowess of California was not yet a factor because, who wanted to be a farmer when there were such riches to be made as a prospector?

The first problem that was faced in creating a major agricultural presence in the islands was the lack of land. Almost all of the land in Hawai'i at this time was occupied by the ali'i, and few Hawaiians were interested in becoming large scale export farmers. The missionaries owned some small holdings that they had been granted over the years. The only other haoles with any land had married into royal families, such as John Parker who founded the huge cattle ranch on Hawai'i. Pressure had been placed on the monarchy to sell land for many years, but it was steadfastly resisted. If you recall from earlier discussions, the monarchy owned all of the land, with ali'i only having historical use of the lands that they occupied.

This was all to change with the Great Mahele of 1848. From their first arrival Americans had been pressuring the monarchy to become more democratic. From the time of Kamehameha leases and simple use of land was granted to Westerners for service rendered to the kingdom. However, they were never given a title or deed to the land. The new constitution of 1840 had also loosened up restrictions on land use and leasing, but the ancient system of the monarchy possessing title was not changed until Kauikeaouli, Kamehameha III, issued the Great Mahele. Under this system one-third of the land, called crown lands, was retained by the monarchy. One-third would be available to the ali'i, and one-third would be available to commoners. With this ownership came the right to buy and sell the land. The ali'i had the opportunity to buy the land that they were already occupying under the old feudal system. They could pay this tax by relinquishing some of their holdings back to the monarchy. They were free to do as they chose with their remaining land. Since the days of the sandalwood trade the ali'i often found themselves in debt and the opportunity to sell land was very tempting. Some of the more unscrupulous Westerners also used technicalities to cheat the Hawaiians out of their land.

The case with commoners was different. They had to fill out a few forms and pay a very reasonable tax called a kuleana to obtain title to a small three acre tract of land. It should be kept in mind that, with the long growing season and fertile soil, it was possible to grow enough food to feed a family in comfort on this amount of land. The goal of this policy was to make Hawai'i a land of small farmers. Unfortunately, few commoners went to the trouble of registering their land. In fact, many didn't have the money to pay the tax. It should be noted that, as with other indigenous people like American Indians, the concept of land ownership was foreign to their frame of reference. They used the land to meet their needs but had no interest in holding a deed to it.

Land was opened up for sale to foreigners in 1850. To the Westerners, with their quest for land ownership, this was a golden opportunity. Within a period of 30 years Westerners owned 80% of the private land, rendering the Hawaiians basically a landless people. This is part of the reason for the popularity of the present sovereignty movement. But that is another story to be told later in this book.

Many of the descendants of the American missionaries went into business. After the decline of the whaling industry they became active in supplying the machinery and general supplies that were needed by the sugar plantations. This naturally led to their involvement in the shipping industry. In an island nation the importance of shipping is paramount to any business activity. The raw sugar needed to be refined and Californian Claus Spreckels bought up a high percentage of the crop for refinement in his mills. In a short time he was even growing his own sugar on Maui. The missionary descendants soon became involved in banking so that they would have the financial resources to tie it all together. As the poorly managed sugar plantations fell into debt they were taken over by these trading companies. Some plantations were even muscled out of business by high shipping rates and high interest loans. These holding companies would make money even in years when the sugar prices were down, which was not unusual. The most powerful of these companies came to be known as the "Big Five". The Big Five were Castle and Cooke, C.Brewer, Alexander and Baldwin, Theo Davies & Co., and American Factors (Am Fac). The 19th century headquarters of these giants of finance can still be visited in downtown Honolulu.

The Big Five were all linked together by intertwining boards of directors. This made them a virtual monopoly that could not be challenged. They were the primary force behind the Great Mahele and its main beneficiaries. Since they had long standing roots in the community they came to be the trusted advisors of the monarchy. The monarchs clearly needed counsel in dealing with business relations with outside interests. The members of the Big Five were only too willing to provide this service, which of course also served to give them the inside track in all business ventures.

A number of constitutions were drafted by the monarchy to deal with their changing relationships with both the commoners and foreign influences. A constant pressure was exerted to force the government in the direction of a representative democracy. A two chamber legislature was formed that contained elements of both the British parliament and the U.S. Congress. This was fitting as the influence of these two countries was the dominant outside pressure on the monarchy. Kamehameha leaned strongly toward the British. His successors swayed to one direction then another, but the omnipresent influence of the missionaries and their descendants, who were largely educated in America, could leave little doubt as to which power would ultimately prevail.

A good example of American influence in the islands was the American Reciprocity Act of 1874. In return for allowing Hawaiian sugar to be imported duty free the United States got the use of Pearl Harbor as a naval base. This agreement gave Hawaiian sugar a very competitive price position in the States and gave the U.S. Navy perhaps the finest harbor facility in the Pacific Ocean. The ties were only to grow closer as commerce weaved the two countries into a complex trade network with financial benefits for both.

Let us now examine the labor needs of the sugar industry. Both sugar and pineapple, which began to be grown commercially in the late 1800's, are labor intensive crops. In addition to requiring intensive hand labor, both crops require physically demanding work in a hot climate. Needless to say, there were few people eager to take these jobs. As you would expect, the Hawaiian people were the first labor source to be tried. The Islanders did not like working in the cane fields and were accustomed to a more laid back lifestyle. They were able to feed and shelter themselves without working the regimented shifts required by the plantations.

The first outside labor force to be imported were Chinese coolies brought to the islands in 1852. They were hired directly from China on five year contracts. They were provided living quarters and limited food and clothing allowances. If they refused to work to the plantation owner's satisfaction, they would be jailed until they changed their attitude. Most of the Chinese did not enjoy plantation life and left the plantations as soon as their contracts were completed, returning to China with their savings. This capital would be sufficient to set them up very well in China. Others stayed on in the islands and moved into the cities where many went into business. In short order a Chinatown was forming in Honolulu, and in 1886, of all business licenses issued in Honolulu, 60% went to Chinese individuals. By the late 1800's the Chinese made up approximately one-fourth of the population of Honolulu. Some of these businesses did very well and the resources were available to stimulate other Chinese to go into business. Between 1852 and 1876 many thousands of Chinese were imported. By the time of annexation a total of over 45, 000 Chinese had relocated to the islands.

By the mid 1860's the Chinese outnumbered Caucasians in Hawai'i. This was a source of worry to some of the Westerners who were generally very biased against the Chinese. Another problem with the contract labor system was that it too closely resembled slavery for the likes of some. As slavery was just being abolished in the States it was a topic of heated debates. The issue quickly became moot because of the Chinese Exclusion Act of 1882. Americans placed pressure on Hawaiians to honor this act if they wanted to retain duty free status on their sugar. The Kingdom passed its own exclusion act in 1888 in succumbing to this pressure. The cries of "yellow peril" created a kind of hysteria that was much more pronounced on the mainland than in Hawai'i, which was rapidly developing a multi-cultural character of its own. When the first individual of Chinese ancestry was elected to the Territorial legislature in 1927, this multiculturalism was institutionalized. Hiram Fong, whose father was a Chinese field laborer, put himself through Harvard Law School. He was a court attorney who entered politics and was elected to the U.S. Senate after statehood, showing the degree of acceptance of individuals of various ethnic groups in the islands.

The first Japanese arrived in the islands in 1868, but it was almost 20 years later before widespread migration to Hawai'i from Japan took place. In 1886 the government of Japan, which was experiencing severe overcrowding, was instituting policies to encourage emigration to Hawai'i. The Eta, the lowest class of Japanese, were the focus of these policies. Few Japanese women moved to Hawai'i and the men had the goal of saving up $3,000 from their contracts and then returning to

Japan. Eventually over 180,000 Japanese came to Hawai'i under the contract labor system. These workers were highly valued by the plantation owners because they were obedient, caused few problems, and were considered hard workers.

Early Sugar Workers

As the attitudes of the Japanese plantation workers started to change and they began to see the economic potential in remaining in Hawai'i rather than returning to Japan, many sent back to Japan for "mail order" brides. Though marriage to individuals not of Japanese ancestry was culturally discouraged, many began marrying individuals of different ethnicity which led to the rich cultural mix that composes Hawai'i at present. The second and third generations of AJAs (Americans of Japanese ancestry) were more integrated with Hawaiian society than their parents. Many entered business or set up small truck farms for growing fresh produce on completion of their contracts. Japanese language newspapers such as the Hawaii Hochi were started and attracted many loyal readers.

In the late 1880's another effort was made to bring larger numbers of Hawaiians into the sugar industry. Upon her death, Princess Bernice Pauahi Bishop's will created the Bishop Estate. She was an heir to the Kamehameha dynasty and left thousands of acres of land, one-ninth of the land in Hawaii, to her estate. The land was to be used to generate funds that would benefit Native Hawaiians. To carry out this mandate the Kamehameha Schools were founded in 1887. The emphasis of the training provided by the school was to be vocational agriculture. The Board of Trustees of the estate was composed of haoles, most well connected with the Big Five. It is an interesting side note that the first principal of the school, William Oleson, was one of the leaders of the revolution of 1893. In the early years of the school, alumni complained that they were being short changed by the narrow focus. As more and more graduates went on to college the vocational emphasis was abandoned. All in all the vocational programs at the Kamehameha Schools did not greatly increase the number of Hawaiians going into plantation work.

The last nationality of laborers to be brought over in large numbers from Asia to work the sugar fields were workers from the Philippines. By 1932 over 100,000 Filipinos had been brought in to work in the plantations. The planters sought to keep the Asian immigrants from the various countries separate, encouraged disputes between these groups, and made efforts to keep them from unifying, which would have given the laborers more power. Some groups, such as the Filipinos, were even divided among themselves. Conflicts existed between Tagalog and Ilocano. One of the toughest challenges facing early labor organizers in the islands was getting the various ethnic groups to work together to reach their common goals. In a subsequent chapter the rise of organized labor in the 20th century will be explored.

Immigrants from various European nations were also tried as a labor source. Most of these individuals demanded higher wages and more say in their working conditions, which made them unacceptable to the planters. The only Europeans to come over in considerable numbers were from Portugal. The Portuguese were willing to work for lower wages than other Europeans. Since they were considered closer to the planter's own ethnic background than the Asians, the Portuguese were often put in the role of overseers, or luna, as they were called. Even working in the fields the Portuguese were always paid higher salaries than Asians doing the same labor.

All of the individuals making up the Hawaiian labor force arrived in the islands speaking their own language or dialects. In order to be able to communicate, the universal language of pidgin, with phrases from many languages, evolved. The native Hawaiians picked up pidgin along with their native language and it is still widely spoken on all of the islands by "locals".

Chapter 6
Hawaiian Monarchy

An examination of the Hawaiian government that was operating during the tumultuous changes of the 19th century is now required. Liholiho, who replaced the past unifier of the islands, Kamehameha, called himself Kamehameha II. As stated previously, the wife of the original monarch, Ka'ahumanu, in her role as kuhina nui, was very much running things upon the death of her husband. Liholiho became caught up in the pretenses of royalty and cut quite a handsome figure in his English finery. His wife, Princess Kamamalu, was equally impressive in her ornate gowns and jewelry. Not having much to do in running the government, they decided to take a trip to England to meet the king. Unfortunately, they failed to inform King George of their intended visit and landed without fanfare in Portsmouth in the spring of 1824. Their manners were in serious need of improvement if they were to enter the high style world of life in the English court. While undergoing tutoring in the British social graces, first Kamamalu and then Liholiho caught the measles. This disease, to which the Hawaiians had no natural immunity, often proved fatal in the islands. Even with the advanced medical practices of the British, both king and queen died in the span of a few days. Liholiho drafted a hasty will on his death bed and stated that the throne should go to his younger brother, Kauikeaouli, the last living son of Kamehameha the Great.

Kauikeaouli, Kamehameha III, became king, but Ka'ahumanu remained very much in power. She and other ali'i had petitioned for membership in the church. Hiram Bingham, the minister of Kawaiahao church in Honolulu, placed them on six months probation, but finally admitted them to membership. A large number of commoners quickly followed suit and in a short while Bingham was preaching to crowds of over a thousand. Kauikeaouli, unenthusiastic about church membership, set about undermining the Christians in earnest when Ka'ahumanu died in 1832. He lifted the penalties for adultery and slept with his sister, following ancient tradition. He had already been a saloon keeper and supposedly forced some Christians to drink. He was a patron of the traditional Hawaiian arts and brought back the hula, condemned by the missionaries as a heathen dance. All of these actions caused an uproar among the Christian ali'i. They forced Kamehameha III to renounce these actions and return to the Christian values of Ka'ahumanu in 1835. He took this as a repudiation of his authority and abandoned caring about affairs

Kawaiahao Congregational Church

of state. This allowed foreigners, particularly the missionaries, to greatly increase their power in the kingdom. Little changed in day to day morality, however, which led Mark Twain to state in the 1850's, "sin no longer flourishes here in name, only in reality".

Due to the influence of his haole counselors, Kauikeaouli issued the Declaration of Rights, which gave the foreigners a stronger legal foothold in the Islands. Such inside pressure also led Kamehameha III to proclaim the Great Mahele, which gave foreigners a mechanism for owning land outright in the islands for the first time. Many who had acquired land through intermarriage with prominent ali'i could now greatly expand their holdings by means of purchasing additional acreage.

It was during this period that the British, French, Russians, and Americans were all vying for influence over Hawai'i. A group of Americans pushed for annexation in the late 1840's. This first of many attempts was successfully resisted by Kauikeaouli, but a treaty creating a most favored nation status between the two countries was signed on December 20, 1849. Kamehameha III died in 1854 having overseen the erosion of Hawaiian sovereignty in terms of both domestic and international affairs during his reign, which was the longest of any Hawaiian monarch.

The next king was Alexander Liholiho, Kamehameha IV, an adopted relative of Kamehameha III. While still a teenager he had traveled to the United States and Europe with his brother under the tutelage of Dr. Judd. As a side note, Dr. Judd, who arrived in the islands as a medical missionary, was probably the most influential and trusted advisor of the monarchy. He held the position of Prime Minister for many years as well as serving as financial manager for several kings. Kamehameha IV and his wife, Emma, were great admirers of all things British. They went so far as to try to make the Anglican Church the main religion of Hawai'i. You can imagine how well this was received by the well entrenched Congregationalist missionaries. They created the currently popular jewelry style known as Hawaiian Heritage jewelry. With its old English lettering amid Hawaiian floral patterns it is most distinctive.

These pro-British actions played into the hands of some haoles who wanted closer ties with America. They could again talk of a British threat to the independence of the islands. In actuality, the British had many opportunities to forge tighter bonds with Hawai'i and did not seem all that interested. As with many of his predecessors, the king's health was never strong, and he died in 1863 at the young age of 29.

He was succeeded by his brother Lot, Kamehameha V. King Lot, the last of the Kamehameha line, was a much more forceful ruler than his brother. He wished to restore the power of the monarchy and set out to achieve this goal. Unconcerned with haole influence, Lot's immediate goal was to replace the Constitution of 1852 with a new constitution that would rein in the power of the foreigners, or at least slow down their drive for control. The Hawaiian Legislature during this time period was operating under a particularly unfavorable set of circumstances. Haole members refused to learn Hawaiian while Hawaiian members refused to speak English in the legislative chambers, although they were fluent. It is hard to imagine a less efficient way to run the government. King Lot broke the stalemate by removing power from the legislature altogether and assumed complete control himself. He was, however, careful to create a political climate favorable to business interests. The sugar plantations started to import Asian workers under his reign and profits soared. He was prudent in financial matters and made sure that the government was adequately funded. During his reign Hawai'i reached a favorable balance of trade for the first time in its history. By walking this delicate tightrope he was able to benefit both the monarchy and haole business interests.

Like so many kings before him, Lot died young. A lifelong bachelor, he died on his 40th birthday in 1872. With no clear successor the job of picking the next monarch passed to the legislature. The two leading contenders were David Kalākaua and Prince William Lunalilo, who was derisively called "Whisky Bill" by his detractors. Lunalilo was a charming man who was beloved by Hawaiian commoners. He was elected and promptly appointed Americans to three of the four major cabinet positions. He appeared to be more interested in a good party than in running the government and Hawaiian interests were further undermined. He died after less than two years in office and the process of succession again fell to the legislature.

The main contenders were Queen Emma, Alexander Liholiho's wife, and again David Kalākaua. This time Kalākaua was victorious. This touched off riots by Emma's supporters and the British marines were called in to restore order. Eventually things quieted down and King Kalākaua was able to take up his role as monarch. By this time the haole sugar interests were exerting ever more governmental control, both directly and indirectly. Kalākaua saw this as a threat to his power and tried to exert more autonomy.

He was a great champion of Hawaiian arts in all of their forms. His patronage of the hula in particular was not to the liking of the Christian missionaries who had been trying to stamp out what they viewed as lewd dancing since their arrival in the islands. The resurrection of the hula from near extinction was viewed as such a personal crusade of the monarch that the most prestigious hula festival in the islands, the Merrie Monarch Festival was named after him. One of Kalākaua's projects for improving the status of the monarchy was the creation of a palace worthy of royalty in Honolulu. Iolani Palace, which still stands next to the Hawaiian State

King Kalakaua

Capitol, was the end result of his efforts. The palace, which is the only palace on U.S. soil, has undergone a major renovation during the past decade and is being restored to its previous glory. Many of the sugar planters saw this as an enormous waste of resources, but the Hawaiians clearly disagreed. Along with the trappings of royalty, the king traveled widely with his wife, Queen Kapiolani, to spread knowledge of his kingdom. There were none of the clumsy attempts at social sophistication of earlier monarchs. King Kalākaua was a truly cosmopolitan man who traveled easily in the ranks of royalty. He was particularly well received in the United States, which he saw as the country most integrally involved in the future welfare of his country.

Since the 1840's the power of the monarchy had been limited by a constitution of one form or another. These constitutions varied in both scope and power, depending on the nature of the monarch in power, and the relationship of the monarch with the moneyed interests who saw the constitutions as giving at least a measure of security to their Hawaiian investments. Kalākaua's luxurious taste dictated the necessity of maintaining a reasonable relationship with the moneyed interests. Against his better judgment he agreed to a new constitution in 1887 that transferred more power from the king to the legislature. Hawaiian resentment against this constitution, called the "Bayonet Constitution" for the force used to get the King to sign it, caused an escalation of tension that would come to a head under the next monarch. King Kalākaua died while on a trip to San Francisco in 1891. He was succeeded by his sister, Queen Liliuokalani, the last of the Hawaiian monarchs.

Upon coming to power Liliuokalani made the abolition of the 1887 constitution and restoration of power to the monarchy her major goals. She was far less willing to compromise than her brother had been. Her interests were diametrically opposed by a growing number of Americans who were interested in Hawai'i becoming a U.S. territory. She was overthrown in a largely bloodless revolution in 1893. This revolution will be covered in detail in the next chapter.

Chapter 7
Revolution

As the sugar companies became ever more powerful they became less and less willing to allow the power of the monarchy to remain unchecked. After rising to the throne at the age of 52, Queen Liliuokalani moved quickly to revoke the constitution of 1887, which her brother had signed under duress. She was aware of the potential danger of eliminating this constitution, but underestimated the power of the planters and merchants. She also wished to replace all of her haole ministers with Hawaiians.

Many of the Americans in the Islands found this threatening and a dozen of them, led by Lorrin Thurston, formed the Annexation Club. Many of the members of this club, including Thurston, became the nucleus of the Committee of Safety to be mentioned later. While he was in Washington, Thurston set up a secret meeting with President Harrison. He was given verbal assurances that Harrison favored annexation. The legislature of 1892 was more chaotic than usual. The followers of the Queen wanted a constitutional convention to draft a new constitution which would restore power to the royalty. The followers of Thurston, on the other hand, were pushing for a constitution that would speed the path to annexation. With all of this infighting essential matters, such as appropriation bills, were ignored. Liliuokalani, in a measure that was far ahead of its time, backed a bill to create a national lottery as a revenue source. A less enlightened bill that would have licensed and legalized opium was also proposed. Maintaining hopes of bankrupting the country and thus forcing annexation, the Queen's adversaries opposed all revenue bills. The Queen appointed her seventh cabinet of the year amid a storm of controversy.

A new constitution was then proposed by the Queen. Two of its major features were that only true Hawaiians could vote, and property qualifications for voting would be removed. Liliuokalani was well aware of the potential ramifications of this new constitution. She postponed announcing the new constitution as she feared that it could very well lead to a haole revolution.

News of the constitution was leaked and the Americans made their move. Thurston and his friends were convinced

Lorrin Thurston

that the Queen would soon ruin the country. A Committee of Safety was formed and they began drafting papers for a provisional government on January 15, 1893. The Queen went to the U.S. Minister Stevens to see if he would back the monarchy, but he had been meeting in secret with the conspirators already and would give her no assurances. Several hundred supporters of the Queen gathered in the Palace Square to voice their support. A crowd of 1,500 gathered to hear what the Committee of Safety had to say. Tensions remained high and the following Monday four boatloads of troops from the U.S. Boston entered Honolulu under orders from Stevens. Sanford Dole, head of the Supreme Court, became president of the provisional government. The Committee of Safety then took possession of the government buildings and the new government was recognized by Minister Stevens. Liliuokalani, wishing to avoid bloodshed, resigned and the revolution was complete.

The annexationists, including Thurston, traveled to Washington to ask for territorial status, but the administration had changed and Grover Cleveland, a democrat, was now president. Cleveland put them on hold and sent his own delegate to Hawai'i to research the revolution. John Blount, a former Congressman, was wined and dined by the Big Five. They assumed that he would naturally take their side, but he gathered over 1,000 pages of testimony from a broad cross section of Hawaiians. He urged Cleveland not to sign the annexation treaty and to reject the claims of Thurston and his allies that they represented the people of Hawai'i.

Based on a careful assessment of Blount's report Cleveland made a speech to Congress on December 18, 1893. Here are some excerpts from that speech.

To the Senate and House of Representatives:
"As I apprehend the situation, we are brought face to face with the following conditions:

The lawful Government of Hawai'i was overthrown without the drawing of a sword or the firing of a shot by a process every step of which, it may be safely asserted, is directly traceable to and dependent for its success upon the agency of the United States acting through its diplomatic and naval representatives.

But for the notorious predilections of the United States Minister for annexation, the Committee of Safety, which should be called the Committee of Annexation, would never have existed.

But for the landing of the United States forces upon false pretexts respecting the danger to life and property the committee would never have exposed themselves to the pains and penalties of treason by undertaking the subversion of the Queen's Government.

But for the presence of the United States forces in the immediate vicinity and in position to afford all needed protection and support the committee would not have proclaimed the provisional government from the steps of the Government building.

And finally, but for the lawless occupation of Honolulu under false pretexts by the United States forces, and but for Minister Stevens' recognition of the provisional government when the United States forces were its sole support and constituted its only military strength, the Queen and her Government would never have yielded to the provisional government, even for a time and for the sole purpose of submitting her case to the enlightened justice of the United States.

Believing, therefore, that the United States could not, under the circumstances disclosed, annex the islands without justly incurring the imputation of acquiring them by unjustifiable methods, I shall not again sub-

mit the treaty of annexation to the Senate for its consideration, and in the instructions to Minister Willis, a copy of which accompanies this message, I have directed him to so inform the provisional government.

But in the present instance our duty does not, in my opinion, end with refusing to consummate this questionable transaction. It has been the boast of our government that it seeks to do justice in all things without regard to the strength or weakness of those with whom it deals. I mistake the American people if they favor the odious doctrine that there is no such thing as international morality, that there is one law for a strong nation and another for a weak one, and that even by indirection a strong power may with impunity despoil a weak one of its territory.

By an act of war, committed with the participation of a diplomatic representative of the United States and without authority of Congress, the Government of a feeble but friendly and confiding people has been overthrown. A substantial wrong has thus been done which a due regard for our national character as well as the rights of the injured people requires we should endeavor to repair. The provisional government has not assumed a republican or other constitutional form, but has remained a mere executive council or oligarchy, set up without the assent of the people. It has not sought to find a permanent basis of popular support and has given no evidence of an intention to do so. Indeed, the representatives of that government assert that the people of Hawai'i are unfit for popular government and frankly avow that they can be best ruled by arbitrary or despotic power.

The law of nations is founded upon reason and justice, and the rules of conduct governing individual relations between citizens or subjects of a civilized state are equally applicable as between enlightened nations.

These principles apply to the present case with irresistible force when the special conditions of the Queen's surrender of her sovereignty are recalled. She surrendered not to the provisional government, but to the United States. She surrendered not absolutely and permanently, but temporarily and conditionally until such time as the facts could be considered by the United States. Furthermore, the provisional government acquiesced in her surrender in that manner and on those terms, not only by tacit consent, but through the positive acts of some members of that government who urged her peaceable submission, not merely to avoid bloodshed, but because she could place implicit reliance upon the justice of the United States, and that the whole subject would be finally considered at Washington.

Actuated by these desires and purposes, and not unmindful of the inherent perplexities of the situation nor of the limitations upon my power, I instructed Minister Willis to advise the Queen and her supporters of my desire to aid in the restoration of the status existing before the lawless landing of the United States forces at Honolulu on the 16th of January last, if such restoration could be effected upon terms providing for clemency as *well as justice to all parties concerned.*

In commending this subject to the extended powers and wide discretion of the Congress, I desire to add the assurance that I shall be much gratified to cooperate in any legislative plan which may be devised for the solution of the problem before us which is consistent with American honor, integrity, and morality."

GROVER CLEVELAND
Executive Mansion,
Washington, December 18, 1893 *1.*

Queen Liliuokalani

The provisional government failed to heed President Cleveland's demands. Since their end run for annexation was foiled, they created the Republic of Hawai'i. Their strategy was

1. *http://info@Hawai'i-nation.org/cleveland.html*

to bide their time until Cleveland's term in office ended and they could again apply for annexation when an administration more favorable to their manipulations took office. They set up a constitutional convention to develop a new constitution for Hawai'i. The requirements for membership in the convention were simple: members must pledge support to the provisional government and resist all efforts to restore the monarchy. With this base of delegates there could be little doubt that the new republic would place the haoles firmly in control. It came to pass that over two-thirds of the ministers in the new government were descendants of the Congregational missionaries who first landed 70 years earlier.

Native Hawaiians still held strong feelings of loyalty to the monarchy, and a plan was created to carry out a counter revolution in early 1895. This revolt, led by Robert Wilcox, a part Hawaiian educated in Italy, was doomed from the start. A few arms had been stockpiled by loyal Hawaiians and the Queen was even drawing up a new constitution. Rumors of the plot caused the police force of the Republic to search in earnest for the weapons cache. On January 6 shots were exchanged between police and royalist sympathizers. The police prevailed and the short lived opposition quickly crumbled. The Queen was implicated in the plot and placed under house arrest in Iolani Palace. She was eventually freed, after eight months of confinement, and went to Washington to plead her case.

With the election of the Republican William McKinley as president in 1898, the annexationists felt the tide turning in their favor. The U.S. House and Senate continued their ongoing debate on annexation. Speedy military victories in the Spanish American War created an urge for territorial expansion and this could only have a positive impact on the annexationists. In early July both the House of Representatives and the Senate passed resolutions of annexation. On July 7, 1898, President McKinley signed the resolution. Hawai'i was now a territory of the United States. It has recently come to light that a petition was circulated at the time of annexation and the overwhelming majority of Hawaiians were in favor of the restoration of the monarchy. These Hawaiian royalists created the Home Rule party to run candidates for office under the Territorial framework of government.

Chapter 8
Territorial Days

With the arrival of territorial status U.S. laws were now the supreme law of the land. While the general American assumption exists that the democratic structure of government allows for a far greater degree of individual freedom than would be found under a monarchy, native Hawaiians did not share this view. The framework of government under territorial status is far different from that put in place when a region becomes a state. The Organic Act, passed in June of 1900, established the framework of the Territorial government, and broadened voting rights to include all male citizens, whether they were landowners or not.

There were three major sources of governmental power in the Territory of Hawaii. The first pillar of power was the governor. This position was far different from the role of governor in a state. The governor was not elected by the people, but appointed by the President for a four year term. Sanford B. Dole was selected as territorial governor. He had far more power than the governor of a state. He controlled all appointments to administrative positions, had absolute veto power over the legislature, could not be impeached, and had the authority to place Hawai'i or any part of Hawai'i under martial law at will. It is interesting to note that, even during Democratic administrations in Washington, a Republican or conservative Democrat served as governor until World War II. The interests of the Big Five were always well represented.

The second major player in the territory was the delegate to Congress. This individual represented the territory of Hawai'i in the U.S. Congress. Unable to cast a vote, the delegate served to merely answer questions about the territory and provide interpretation about how a particular piece of legislation might affect Hawai'i. He further acted as a conduit for information to and from Hawai'i, holding meetings to inform islanders about relevant events in Washington, and carrying the concerns of Hawaiians back to Congress.

The delegate to Congress was elected by a majority vote of the citizens of Hawai'i. This was not as democratic as it superficially appeared. Citizens had to demonstrate literacy in the English language in order to be eligible to vote. This tactic, borrowed from the American South, was quite effective in disenfranchising a large number of Hawaiian residents. Furthermore, any candidates who did not have the blessing of the Big Five were not permitted to campaign on the plantations where a large number of Hawai'i's residents lived. The combination of these two factors assured that anyone with a point of view running counter to big business had a tough fight to be elected in Hawai'i. Despite these obstacles, the Home Rule Party's candidate for delegate to Congress, Robert Wilcox, was victorious. His first act as delegate was to introduce a bill that would extend the land policies of the United States to the territory. This included homesteading provisions that the sugar planters found particularly objectionable. None of Wilcox's proposals were taken seriously by Congress and he quickly lost all effectiveness.

The second elected delegate to Congress was Prince Jonah Kuhio. Ironically, he was an heir to the throne of Queen Liliuokalani. He was convinced by Henry Baldwin, of Alexander and Baldwin fame, that by helping the Big Five he was insuring the economic future of the islands and therefore helping the Hawaiian people. With the support of the Big Five he won every election from 1902, when the Home Rule party was swept from office, until his death in 1922. Though Kuhio represented the Republicans who put him in office there remained a tension between them. He typically won close to 90% of the haole vote when running, yet he genuinely cared about the plight of native Hawaiians.

The last source of power in territorial days was the Territorial Legislature. Members were elected by a vote of the people, but as with the vote for delegate to Congress, the franchise issue and plantation campaigning played to the advantage of candidates representing sugar interests. Though some pro-Hawaiian representatives were always elected, the Big Five maintained control of a majority of seats in the legislature. It would be accurate to state that the Republican party ruled the territory, much as the businessmen who overthrew the Queen had ruled between 1893 and 1898 during the days of the Republic of Hawai'i. This is all the more amazing when you consider the fact that two-thirds of the voters were native Hawaiians during the early days of the territory. The fruits of political power were not limited to the Big Five. Others with missionary roots in the islands, such as Walter Dillingham, made their fortunes on land development and other business ventures.

Prince Jonah Kuhio

It has been said that government was controlled from the lounge of the exclusive Pacific Club in Honolulu, where wealthy sugar planters met to plan their strategies for the future of the islands over snifters of brandy and Cuban cigars. The issue of race was never far beneath the surface. Though many of the planters had married into ali'i society in earlier days and therefore had offspring of mixed blood, they considered themselves the blue bloods of Hawai'i. In dealings with Washington they never missed the chance to state their position as the most pro U.S. element in the islands and hence the most stable and dependable. There can be no denying that the United States was a highly racist society at this point in its history, with the white race holding a virtual monopoly on power and status. Southern Senators in particular were fond of using the issue of race against the new territory. The multiethnic nature of the islands undoubtedly delayed the drive for statehood for many years. Against this backdrop it is easy to see why the planters, who maintained a permanent lobbying office in Washington, were able to wield such a disproportionate amount of power.

Labor disputes came under U.S. law with the passage of annexation in 1898. This gave the workers a certain, though limited, degree of autonomy that had previously been lacking. Five thousand Japanese plantation workers went on strike in 1909. The planters had been adroit at pitting one group of workers against another, so early strikes tended to be composed of workers of one nationality. At this time Japanese workers were being paid 25 % less than Portuguese who were working the same number of hours per month. Strike breakers were hired at twice the rate of pay of the Japanese strikers. The strikers were evicted from their plantation homes. This early strike was a failure and the strikers eventually returned to work at their previous wages. Another strike by Japanese workers in 1920 ended with much the same result.

The Filipino Federation of Labor, under its fiery leader, Pablo Manlapit, went on strike at the same time as the second Japanese strike. They refused to coordinate their strikes and met with similar results. Though wages did not increase, working conditions were upgraded. Manlapit led a second strike of 3,000 Filipino workers in 1924. This time the strike was much less peaceful. The Filipinos were armed and attacked the strike breakers. The situation escalated into a full blown riot; sixteen strikers and four policemen were killed. Eventually the national guard was called in. The strike had again failed and Manlapit was expelled from the country.

The National Labor Relations Act was passed in 1935 as part of FDR's New Deal. This piece of legislation guaranteed workers the right to organize and to use collective bargaining to better their wages and working conditions. The courts upheld the constitutionality of the NLRA in 1937, which set the stage for its implementation. A strike in 1937 by Filipino workers finally succeeded and strikers received a 15% pay increase. By this time two-thirds of plantation workers were Filipino, so the effect of the strike was widespread.

The ILWU - International Longshoremen and Warehousemen's Union came to power in 1938. They led a strike against the Matson Line. The Matson Line was the shipping arm of

Early longshoremen in Hawai'i

the Big Five and had a virtual monopoly on all goods coming into and out of Hawai'i. A strike against them had the potential of bringing all trade in the islands to a standstill. The stakes were high and tensions quickly erupted. In Hilo, on the Big Island, the second largest city in Hawai'i, violence flared between strikers, strikebreakers, and the police. Fifty of the strikers were wounded in the ensuing gunfire and the incident was called the "Hilo Massacre". The strike ended as a stalemate and the workers returned to their jobs with no appreciable gains. Despite this setback the ILWU had established itself as a major player in Hawai'i. At around this time the union affiliated with the CIO - Congress of Industrial Organizations. The larger AFL - American Federation of Labor had also made a bid. Due to the fact that the AFL at this point in its history was considered a decidedly pro-white union the CIO won out. Organizing workers in the Islands would have been very difficult if the parent union was perceived as racist.

During World War II, which will be covered in detail in the next chapter, labor disputes were non-existent, as any stoppage of production was viewed as aiding the enemy. This situation was even more dramatic in Hawai'i, which was under martial law from the attack at Pearl Harbor untill the conclusion of the war. Wages were frozen in the islands by the military commander. However, union members were very proud of the role that they played in helping to win the war.

Shortly after the end of the war, in 1945, the ILWU won its bid to organize the plantation workers. They wasted no time in flexing their collective muscle. In September of 1946, plantation workers numbering 21,000 went out on strike. The sugar companies could not withstand this amount of pressure and Castle & Cooke was the first of the Big Five to settle. It was a clear union victory.

Jack Hall, a very colorful figure with distinct leftist leanings, became head of the ILWU in Hawai'i in the mid 40's. He was instrumental in coordinating a second strike against the Matson Line in 1949. Two thousand dock workers walked off the job and nothing entered or left the islands for six months. The strikers again won and the power of labor was clearly established. In his personal life things did not go so smoothly. Hall was called up in front of the Senate Committee on Internal Security. This committee was the Senate version of McCarthy's "red hunting" House Committee on Un-American Activities. As with many of his contemporaries he pleaded the 5th Amendment. At the time this was seen as an admission of guilt and he was arrested and tried on charges under the Smith Act. This act dealt with charges of teaching the overthrow of the United States government using force and violence. Though he was eventually cleared and never abandoned by loyal union members, it created a blot on his reputation that he never fully overcame. It should be admitted that many labor leaders in Hawai'i flirted with communism during the 30's and 40's. They were pushing for increased rights for workers and minority members, however, and were in no way involved in plots to overthrow the government of the United

States or to ally themselves with the government of the USSR.

Hall's power within the union remained unchallenged and in 1958 he led another strike of sugar workers. The union again won concessions from the planters, setting the stage for a period of relative cooperation between unions and management, since the planters were forced to recognize that they no longer maintained sole control. It would also be fair to speculate that the better standards of working conditions and wages that the plantation workers won in the second half of the 20th century played a role in the massive closure of sugar and pineapple operations that has been taking place during the 1990's. By 1998 there was not a single active sugar mill on the Island of Hawai'i. Dole abandoned Lana'i for cheaper production costs in South East Asia. The remaining sugar and pineapple operations mainly cater to tourists who have an interest in observing the former mainstay of the Hawaiian economy.

Chapter 9
World War II

You are well aware that the United States entered the Second World War with the bombing of Pearl Harbor on December 7, 1941. However, you may not be aware of the long term effects of that attack on the Hawaiian Islands. The attack was not as much of a surprise as we have been led to believe. The military was well aware of the fact that Hawai'i was a prime

Honolulu Star-Bulletin 1st EXTRA

WAR !

(Associated Press by Transpacific Telephone)

SAN FRANCISCO, Dec. 7.—President Roosevelt announced this morning that Japanese planes had attacked Manila and Pearl Harbor.

OAHU BOMBED BY JAPANESE PLANES

target of the Japanese as they expanded their empire in the Pacific. There was a high degree of military preparedness in general in the islands that included close surveillance of any AJAs whose loyalty could be considered suspect.

One of the new technologies being developed as the U.S. moved ever closer to war was radar. Both permanent and mobile radar stations had been set up in Hawai'i in anticipation of an air attack. However, the technology was not perfected and was considered somewhat unreliable by some in the military. At seven a.m. on that Sunday morning two privates manning one of the mobile stations picked up a large concentration of aircraft. Neither man had previously seen this large a number of planes. The planes were incoming approximately 140 miles northwest of the islands. When the planes reached 120 miles out they called in a warning. The switchboard operator had difficulty locating an officer to respond to the privates. When an officer was eventually located he stated that either the planes were on maneuvers from Hickam Air Base on O'ahu or they were a large flight of inbound B-17s from the mainland. The later supposition is hard to take seriously as the planes were approaching from the west.

The Japanese could not have picked a more opportune time to attack. After a long Saturday night of partying in Honolulu many of the troops would not have been at their sharpest on an early Sunday morning. The Japanese planes reached their primary target of Pearl Harbor at five minutes before eight. Secondary targets at Hickam Field and the Army post, Schofield Barracks, also quickly came under attack. The warnings of the radar operators and the four a.m. sighting of a periscope by a mine sweeper off Pearl Harbor had both been ignored and the U.S. forces were caught by surprise. The results of the attack are well documented: 3,435 U.S. casualties, eight battleships and ten other large ships severely damaged, and 188 planes destroyed. The Japanese lost 29 planes and five midget subs that had been trying to blockade the entrance of the harbor to prevent the U.S. ships from escaping. It was an extreme bit of luck that all of the U.S. aircraft carriers were at sea at the time of the attack. These same carriers later were able to win a major naval battle when the Japanese navy was dealt a blow from which they never recovered off Midway Island at the far western end of the Hawaiian Archipelago.

The immediate effect of the attack on Pearl Harbor was rapid preparations for a land invasion by the Japanese. Many thought that the air attack was a precursor for a land assault on the islands within a few days. General Short ordered Governor Poindexter to declare martial law. The Governor called the president who had appointed him, FDR, to get his advice. Roosevelt agreed that he should comply with the order. He further stated that martial law would be short lived if there was no invasion. This turned out to be extremely inaccurate, as martial law remained in effect for the duration of the war, long after there was any real threat to Hawai'i. Poindexter was replaced by a military governor and the civilian government was stripped of all power. The military wielded enormous power during this period. They censored the press, froze wages and set the hours of work, controlled rents, regulated restaurants and bars, declared curfews and blackouts, and replaced the local courts with military tribunals with no writ of *habeus corpus*. These acts were blatant violations of the rights of Hawaiian citizens, but to criticize these measures was considered unpatriotic. The powerful sugar planters wasted no time in inviting high ranking military officers to their social events. In a short period of time the Big Five insured that they would be serving as advisors to the military which reinforced their influence over the islands.

One of the first problems facing the military government was what to do about the 160,000 individuals of Japanese ancestry living in Hawai'i. This was a much more complex issue than measures that were taken to deal with AJA's on the West Coast of the United States. In the first place there was no facility that could possibly be used to inter even one-third of these people in the islands. With the setback that the navy suffered at Pearl Harbor, neither the ships nor time required to move large numbers of these Americans of Japanese ancestry to the mainland could be spared. Furthermore, many AJA's provided labor that was highly skilled and considered essential to the economic wellbeing of the islands.

Most of these AJA's were patriotic Americans. The only group of Japanese in Hawai'i with mixed patriotism were the first generation of Japanese, referred to as issei, who had migrated to Hawai'i . A small group of the older issei men had sympathy with Japan, though they would never admit it publicly. The second generation, called nisei, were very patriotic Americans, often refusing to even speak Japanese with their parents. They would not wear Japanese clothing and asked their mothers to burn their kimonos. They also asked their parents to remove Japanese shrines from their gardens and homes. In denying their heritage they searched for a niche in this new society. These young nisei went down to the recruiting office to sign up in large numbers shortly after the attack on Pearl Harbor. Not only would the recruiters not accept their applications, but the nisei currently enrolled in ROTC programs were dismissed from these positions as well. Japanese Americans who were already members of the National Guard could not legally be dismissed. The military, however, wanted them off the islands as soon as possible. They did not want them present if there was a Japanese invasion. These individuals were shipped out to Wisconsin and reorganized as the 100th Infantry.

In January of 1943, the nisei were finally allowed to enlist. A new battalion, the 442nd Infantry, was created. These young men knew that they would only be allowed to fight in the European theater. The turn out was tremendous. Four thousand volunteered during the first week and 9,000 had enrolled within a month. Three thousand of these applicants were selected for membership in the 442nd. The 100th, like the 442nd, was destined to fight only against the Germans and Italians. They were finally given a combat assignment in 1943 and were sent to join the North African campaign, just as the tide was turning against the famous German General Rommel. They played a major role in the invasion of Italy which shortly followed. They were involved in heavy fighting to capture Rome after German troops were sent to reinforce the rapidly failing Italian army. At this juncture they were joined by the 442nd. The two units fought against very heavy odds in the Northern Italian campaign where the Germans had determined to draw the line. They suffered casualty rates that were three times higher than the army average. The soldiers fought valiantly and ended up the two most decorated units in the history of the U.S. Army. They returned to Hawai'i as heroes and became some of the key players in a political revolution that has influenced the government of Hawai'i to the present day.

Chapter 10
Statehood

The political power of the Big Five was not able to withstand the winds of change that were blowing through Hawai'i following the conclusion of the Second World War. Like African-American war heroes returning from the war who pushed the civil rights movement into high gear when they refused to accept their former roles, the returning Hawaiians were no longer willing to settle for second class citizenship.

Senator Daniel Inouye

Like veterans throughout the United States, many of the returning nisei, went to college on the GI Bill. The fields of law, medicine, and teaching were particularly attractive to the Hawaiian veterans. A young man of great ambition, who came to represent the hopes and dreams of the returning nisei was

Dan Inouye. He had lost his arm in the fighting in Europe and returned home with a chest full of medals, a true hero. After the war he received his law degree from George Washington University and returned to Hawai'i, where he became a key player in the evolving political scene. He was elected to the territorial House of Representatives and became the majority leader when the Democrats swept to power in 1955. He was the first AJA to be elected to the U.S. House of Representatives in 1959, when Hawai'i had its first election after statehood. He has since been elected to the U.S. Senate where he still maintains his seat as the senior Senator from Hawai'i.

Two major players arose to fight for several years for control of the Democratic party in Hawai'i. The first was Jack Hall, the head of the ILWU, who you have already met in the chapter on labor. The long history of organized labor's ties to the Democratic party would set Hall up as a natural key player as the party rose to power. His supposed links to the Communist party, though they garnered major headlines in Hawaiian newspapers, did little to dim his popularity. His opponent for control of the party was Jack Burns. Burns came up through the ranks of the party over the years. He was a detective in the Honolulu police department and thus was no stranger to the less affluent population of O'ahu. His ties with "the street" were a great value to him throughout his political tenure. He was known as a champion of the common man, whereas Hall's base was almost exclusively in organized labor. Burns developed particularly strong ties within Honolulu's Chinese and Japanese districts. After the war he was the first to capitalize on the emerging political power of Americans of Chinese and Japanese ancestry. He took many of the young Japanese seeking office, such as Dan Inouye and Patsy Mink, under his wing and helped them to launch their careers. This created a loyal group of followers as he began his bid to gain control of the Democratic party. Burns and Hall both tried to gain control of the 1948 state Democratic Convention. Neither man was able to garner a majority of delegates but collectively they were able to unseat the "old guard" of the party. Both men were wise enough to recognize that nothing was to be gained by undermining the constituency of the other. A coalition was formed without a clear leader. However, at the 1952 convention Burns gained control, with the shifting support of organized labor, and Hall refocused his energies on labor concerns, remaining a strong behind-the-scenes player in Hawaiian politics for years to come.

The now unified Democratic party took on the Republicans who had held a virtual monopoly on governmental power in Hawai'i since annexation. The elections in 1954 were the turning point. Democrats won two-thirds of the seats in the House of the territorial legislature and almost as large of a percentage in the Senate. They have held similar or larger majorities in almost every legislature up to the present day. It was during this same decade of the 50's that the issue of Statehood would finally be resolved. When Hawai'i was annexed in 1898 it was never assured future statehood. No offshore territory had ever been granted statehood. Some said that Hawai'i would challenge the "Western traditions" of the United States. Early in his political career, Strom Thurmond of South Carolina stated, "the U.S. is the maximum development of Western culture - at the opposite extreme is Eastern culture which is dominant in Hawai'i". He then quoted Kipling, "East is East and West is West, and never the twain shall meet". Some Southern congressmen stated that Hawai'i was populated by individuals of dubious ethnic stock. They surmised, and not incorrectly, that congressmen from Hawai'i would be liberal, particularly in matters of racial affairs.

Hawai'i created a Statehood Commission to keep the push for statehood on the agenda in Washington. Some of the facts that they presented in the early 50's are as follows. Hawai'i paid more taxes to the U.S. government than nine existing states, yet had no voice in how the money was spent. The population at this time was half a million, which was more than four existing states. Hawai'i had a larger population than any territory except Oklahoma at the time of statehood. Nine out of ten residents of the Islands were citizens - to counter the Asian influence argument. Almost every major power group in Hawai'i was in favor of statehood. In 1940, during the first election in which Hawaiian citizens voted on the issue, voters favored statehood by a margin of three to one. Some of those opposed to statehood were native Hawaiians who contended that the monarchy had been illegally overthrown and therefore they desired no closer links with the United States.

On the U.S. mainland a poll in 1946 showed that six out of ten were in favor of statehood for Hawai'i. By 1954 this majority had risen to 78%. Every Hawaiian delegate to the U.S. Congress since 1936 had introduced statehood resolutions to the Congress. When Jack Burns was elected as delegate to Congress for the first time in 1948, the number one item on his agenda was statehood. He crafted and lobbied for countless statehood bills. As with many other issues, the admission of Hawai'i as a state took on partisan overtones. It was clear to Republicans in Congress that Hawai'i would tend to elect Democrats to Congress. It was a correct assumption, as almost every Hawaiian Senator and Representative in the House has been a Democrat during the 40 years since statehood. Indeed, the overwhelming success of the party in Hawai'i in the early 50's was a force which proved detrimental to the fight for statehood. Southern Democrats in both houses of Congress were prime opponents of statehood, as they had been opponents of annexation 60 years earlier. Any diehard segregationist was correct in opposing Hawai'i, as the Hawaiian delegation after statehood was one of the prime supporters of subsequent civil rights legislation in the 1960's. Hawaii's Congressional delegation has become famous as being progressive on many social issues and not just civil rights.

In the second half of the 1950's a rivalry developed between Alaska and Hawai'i in a virtual race for statehood. There were several similarities between the two territories. Both were not connected directly to the contiguous 48 states, and both territories had large numbers of non-white residents. Delegations from both territories quickly realized that if the other territory were admitted to statehood first it would place increased pressure on Washington to admit the second. It was decided that Hawai'i would not stand in the way of Alaska's being first, and the two territories joined ranks and shared common lobbying strategies.

Under continued pressure Southern Democrats began to soften their position, and Hawai'i's strategic military position appealed to some mainland Republicans. The House of Representatives was the first to pass a statehood bill in February of 1959. The Senate followed with a similar bill on March 11th.

President Eisenhower, a longstanding supporter of statehood for Hawai'i, signed the legislation on March 18, 1959.

Now all that was needed was for the citizens of Hawai'i to ratify these congressional votes. A special election was held on June 27. Hawaiians ratified statehood by a margin of 17 to 1. The only precinct voting against statehood was the small island of Ni'ihau, which was composed entirely of native Hawaiians. Hawai'i became the 50th state amid widespread celebration in the new Aloha State.

The first matter to be resolved was the composition of Hawai'i's delegation to Congress and the election of a governor. Special elections were held in the fall. It surprised no one when Dan Inouye won election to Hawai'i's single seat in the House of Representatives. What surprised some was that Jack Burns did not run for the Senate, but decided to stay in Hawai'i and join the race for Governor. More surprising yet was his defeat by Republican William Quinn, a former territorial Governor. Burns was to get his revenge, however, as he defeated Quinn in 1962 and served a total of three terms as Governor.

Democrats were to control both houses of the state legislature and the office of governor for the next 40 years. This lengthy monopoly on power was ended in 2002 with the election of Republican Linda Lingle as governor. It was widely perceived that the Democrats had been in power for such a long period of time that widespread corruption was inevitable. Apparently the dissatisfaction was far from a sweeping movement when voters again elected a Democratic majority to both houses of the state legislature as well as maintaining the all Democratic Hawai'i delegation to the United States Congress.

Governor Linda Lingle

Chapter 11
Economic Restructuring

With the arrival of statehood, and the increased democratization of power in the islands when the the Big Five lost control, some were thrilled to proclaim the arrival of a "new Hawai'i". Others contended that the new coalition presided over by Governor Burns and his allies was no more democratic than the near feudal system that it had replaced. As in all political systems there was an element of "to the victors go the spoils". However, unlike the old system, the people had the ballot box as a mechanism to voice displeasure should the new system get too far out of line.

In 1969, on the tenth anniversary of statehood, Governor Burns created the Conference on the Year 2000 Committee to chart a long range plan for the next 30 years. One of the subjects being studied was race. One of the statistics that came out of the study was that Hawai'i had by far the highest percentage of interracial marriages in the United States, approaching 50%. This was used to reinforce the image of Hawai'i as a melting pot. Another hot topic was the displacement of native Hawaiians from the land, particularly on O'ahu and Maui. Young people in particular expressed a great deal of skepticism about the whole Year 2000 project. The notion of aloha was brought into question. Was it just a tourism marketing tool or was there a real feeling of sharing and concern for others? All in all the committee raised more questions than it answered, but it was a rare study of democracy in action.

The major driving force in the new Hawai'i was the changing economy rather than the new political system. The decline of the sugar industry, followed shortly by reduced pineapple production, created an economic environment ripe for a new source of revenue. Luckily for the islands, tourism was expanding to more than make up for the lost income. The number of visitors to Hawai'i increased from 40,000 in 1950 to 175,000 by the time of statehood. The boom continued as numbers increased to 1.2 million by 1968 and over 7 million by

1990. Economic problems in Asia during the 90's led to a slow down in total tourism growth in the late 1990's. By 1970 this sector of the economy was contributing more than $ 1 billion dollars yearly, over four times the value of the combined income from all forms of agriculture. The contribution of tourism rose to $10 billion by 1992 and the maximum potential is hard to guess.

Early Waikiki and Diamond Head

Several factors accounted for the tremendous growth of tourism. Before the Second World War, tourists made their way to the islands on expensive cruises with the Matson Line. The line built the first hotels on Waikiki Beach to create a destination resort for these travelers. With the growth of the airline industry tourism grew, but it was the development of large capacity, high speed jets that allowed the masses to escape to the tropics. Many GIs who had spent R&R time in Hawai'i during the war joined the first waves of tourists to return to the islands in large numbers. The increase in disposable income spurred by U.S. economic growth was also a contributing factor.

The tourist boom fueled a second boom, that of the construction industry. The infrastructure needed to support this volume of visitors was tremendous. Not only did hotels appear at an amazing rate in the former swamp that was Waikiki, but resorts were built from scratch in regions not even accessible by road a few years previous to their development. In a state with a powerful and well established system of labor unions this insured a large number of good paying jobs. All of the support industries, from concrete plants to architecture firms, were carried along on this great wave of prosperity. The construction boom carried on in high gear until the slow down of the early 90's.

Hawai'i's growth was not limited to tourists. The resident population, drawn by the booming economy as well as the desire to escape winter, increased dramatically in the decades following statehood. The population was right at a half million in 1950, and nearly 650,000 by statehood. By the early 1990's this population had doubled, but growth has slowed since that juncture. Projections put the population approaching two million by 2020.

The demand for land on which to build this myriad of new tropical oases led to the real estate boom that has also been a major contributing factor to the economy. Unfortunately, this boom has put home ownership out of reach for large numbers of Hawaiians. In an island environment the amount of land is physically limited in ways that mainlanders have difficulty comprehending. Land prices are necessarily very high in proportion to its scarcity. Of the 64% of Hawaiian land that is privately owned, a high percentage is held by a small number of investors such as the Bishop Estate. This places even greater restrictions on the amount of land that is available for sale at any given time. With the limited number of landowners, development has mainly been undertaken by hui. This is a Hawaiian term for a group of investors. Many of the hui that developed in the decades after statehood were controlled by individuals of Chinese ancestry. By withholding land from development the prices could be raised to even higher levels. This has created an environment in which many of the original Hawaiian inhabitants of the islands are unable to buy land in their own homeland.

The red hot Japanese economy in the early 90's created a massive inflow of yen that drove land prices, particularly in the Honolulu area, to astronomical levels. A simple three bedroom tract house could be valued at one-third of a million dollars. While the market has slowed down dramatically since that period, land will never be cheap in paradise.

The geographic location of Hawai'i in the middle of the Pacific basin has always played a major role in the economy of the region. This Asian link has been further developed by the creation of the East-West Center, developed in affiliation with the University of Hawai'i in Honolulu. The center was established in 1960 to provide an academic think tank to examine the potential relationship between Hawai'i and the Pacific Rim. The recent decline in the value of the yen and the general slowdown of the Asian tigers has decreased Asian investment in Hawai'i, but the strategic location of the islands and the mulicultural makeup of the population creates a natural environment for economic partnerships between Asia and this westernmost state in the United States.

With the withdrawal of most sugar and pineapple plantations from the islands much agricultural land has been opened up for alternative uses. The last sugar mill on the Big Island closed in the late 1990's and Dole Pineapple eliminated their agricultural operations from the island of Lana'i in the 90's as well. Since they controlled the entire island, it has created the opportunity to redesign the island for alternative uses. This has lead to an increase in what is termed diversified agriculture. Some of the major crops that are currently being grown for export are papaya, macadamia nuts, and coffee. All three of these crops have increased dramatically in the last ten years. Kona coffee, which is grown at mid-elevations on the leeward coast of the Big Island, is considered one of the finest coffees in the world. Sunrise papayas from the Puna region on the windward coast of Hawai'i are now finding international markets. Macadamia nuts from Hilo are replacing pineapple in many suitcases as the food gift of choice for friends overseas. Floriculture has emerged as another major agricultural focus of the islands. The orchids, anthuriums, gingers, and other cut flowers produced in Hawai'i are exported around the globe. The growing of produce for consumption in the islands is also increasing. Taro, the root crop grown by Kamehameha himself in Waipio Valley, is becoming a more common component of the Hawaiian diet, in the form of poi.

The newest forest product to be grown on old sugar land is eucalyptus trees. These fast growing trees are being marketed as a source of pulp for paper production in Japan. Tropical hardwoods such as koa and ohia are being replanted on upland slopes of Hawai'i's volcanoes. These high value woods can serve as the basis for a woodworking industry that can provide good paying, high skill jobs indefinitely if sustained yield forestry is practiced. A further benefit is habitat restoration to aid the plight of the many Hawaiian plants and animals on the endangered species list.

Hawai'i's natural beauty

Another new agricultural venture in Hawai'i is the growing of timber bamboo. This giant grass exceeds six inches in diameter when mature and has a strength to weight ratio that far surpasses steel. It will become a source of low cost housing material when treatment facilities are completed in the Puna district of the island of Hawai'i.

The twenty world-class observatories on the 13,796 foot summit of Mauna Kea are creating both economic and academic resources for the island of Hawai'i. The dry, clear air at this summit creates viewing opportunities so outstanding that astronomers must schedule viewing times years in advance.

The intangible qualities of Hawai'i that keep it a magnet for tourists and residents alike must be examined and protected if the economy of the islands is to continue in a sustainable fashion. What value do you put on a tropical sunset over a grove of coconut palms? What is the value of a swim in crystal clear waters? The natural beauty of the islands, along with its rich cultural heritage are recognized by many as the factors that give Hawai'i its unique appeal. How many tourists and resorts can the islands support without destroying these characteristics?

At the heart of these questions lies another question. Is Hawai'i truly developing an independent, self-sustaining economy or is it controlled by outside investors who have merely replaced the planters as the movers and shakers of Hawai'i? While there are no simplistic answers to these worthy questions, there are some rays of hope. For example, there is a tax on all real estate sales in Hawai'i in which the seller is not a resident of Hawai'i. While not eliminating land speculation, this law encourages ownership by residents. And measures are being taken to increase native Hawaiian land ownership, as will be examined in more detail in the final chapter. Immersion programs in the Hawaiian language have been established in many schools to encourage the growth of traditional Hawaiian culture.

It is not the purview of historians to predict the future. However, an examination of the Hawaiian sovereignty movement will be the concluding chapter. This growing movement will undoubtedly have a profound effect on the shape of Hawai'i in the new millennium.

Chapter 12
Sovereignty

One of the unforeseen offshoots of the boom in tourism was an increasing value placed upon Hawaiian art, dance, and music. Visitors view this culture as exotic and this provides a commercial impetus for Hawaiians to revive their culture. Hawaiian culture was now suddenly in high demand. The ensuing Hawaiian renaissance did not stop at mere reenactments to create photo opportunities for tourists. Getting in touch with their roots is a legitimate interest of many native Hawaiians. It should not be surprising that one of the results of this revival is a renewed demand for increased autonomy.

Along with the tourists came the deluge of new residents. Inevitably the demands for land for development from these groups would lead to the displacement of even more Hawaiians from the land. On O'ahu a group called Kokua Kalama was formed in the early 1970's to protest yet one more eviction. The group sparked a rise in activism that has continued to grow since that time. A group with an apt acronym A.L.O.H.A.- Aboriginal Lands of Hawaiian Ancestry- was formed in 1972, with the goal of protesting the overthrow of the monarchy nearly a century earlier.

One of the models that native Hawaiians examined in pressing their claims was the Alaska Native Claims Settlement Act created in 1970. This act had been drafted in the new state to deal with the rights of native Alaskans and resulted in large cash, as well as land settlements to the original inhabitants. It is ironic that the much earlier Hawaiian Homelands Act of 1920 had served as a model for the Alaskans during their deliberations.

The Hawaiian Homelands were established with 188,000 acres to create opportunities for homesteading by Native Hawaiians. Unfortunately much of the acreage that was put into the program was too arid for agriculture. Many of the best acres were leased out rather than made available for homesteads. By 1992 only 40,000 of the acres were being utilized for their original purpose. At that time there was still a waiting list of almost 25,000 Hawaiians seeking land. In order for much of the land to be usable, major expenditures needed to be made for reliable water supplies and utilities.

The Office of Hawaiian Affairs was created in 1978 by an amendment to the state constitution. Its purpose was to hold title to the land given to the state from the federal government at statehood. At annexation, in 1898, the United States had taken possession of the former crown and government lands of the monarchy. This land was established as a trust for native Hawaiians. In the midst of growing internal pressure a commission was created in 1983 by the federal government to study the issue of reparations to native Hawaiians. The commission examined little evidence beyond blatantly pro-American accounts of early Hawaiian history, and ruled against reparations. This announcement was greeted by a storm of indignation from a broad spectrum of Hawaiians including the now powerful Senator Dan Inouye.

Incidents with homeless Hawaiians who moved into tent cities on beaches throughout the islands grabbed a great deal of media attention during the early 1990's. Rents were skyrocketing at this time and people were being evicted in large numbers. These individuals, who were referred to as the "beach people", brought the issue of the plight of native Hawaiians to the attention of all in a manner that could not be ignored.

As sovereignty groups with various agendas proliferated, a Constitutional Convention for a Hawaiian Nation was called in 1987. Representatives from all of the islands came together and drafted a constitution. They also elected Mililani Trask to the position of president of Ka Lahui Hawai'i, The Hawaiian Nation.

In 1993, as the 100th anniversary of the overthrow of the monarchy approached, many groups thought that the time was right for a major push for sovereignty. The federal government gave these groups a great deal of ammunition with the passage of Public Law 103-150. This law, which President Clinton signed in November of 1993, was a formal apology to native Hawaiians from the government of the United States for the overthrow of the monarchy 100 years earlier. The law had extensive quotes from the report of President Cleveland to Congress, included in an earlier chapter of this book.

With all of these demands for change, the previously mentioned Office of Hawaiian Affairs has joined the battle to empower the native people of Hawai'i. However, since the OHA is funded by the state legislature and is in fact an agency of the state of Hawai'i it is viewed by some of the sovereignty activists as having an inherent conflict of interest with efforts to free Hawaiians from state and federal control. OHA's problems were further magnified by a ruling by the Supreme Court of the United States in February, 2000. Harold "Freddy" Rice, a haole rancher whose family has resided in Hawaii since the 1830's, sued the state claiming that OHA elections allowing only native Hawaiians to vote were in violation of the 15th Amendment of the U.S. Constitution which prohibits discrimination in voting based on race. This court ruling in favor of Rice has raised a number of questions that are yet to be resolved. The Governor of Hawaii has declared that all registered voters are eligible to vote for members of the OHA Board as of the November 2000 elections. Non native Hawaiians are also being allowed to run for seats on the OHA Board. The entire base of programs that are designed to provide support for native Hawaiians is now being called into question.

These fears were realized when a lawsuit was filed in September of 2000 in Federal Court on Oahu. This suit filed on behalf of a non-Hawaiian claims the entire Office of Hawaiian Affairs is unconstitutional because it discriminates against non Hawaiians. This suit is being handled by the same attorney who represented Rice in the case cited earlier.

A bill, supported by the Clinton Administration, was introduced into the United States Senate by Hawaiian Senator Daniel Akaka in the Summer of 2000. This bill titled "The Native Hawaiian Recognition Bill" creates a process within the framework of federal law for the Native Hawaiian community to reorganize a governing body for self determination and self-governance. The government to government relationship with the United States created by this bill would be similar to the relationship enjoyed by Native American tribes. The bill is intentionally vague to allow Native Hawaiians to create and elect their own governing body. Once this governing body is in place the U. S. Government can then transfer land, resources and assets dedicated to Native Hawaiians under existing law to the Native Hawaiian Governing Body. This would basically create a new system in which OHA would no longer be needed.

The Hawaiian Sovereignty Advisory Commission, an off-shoot of the OHA, called for a vote in 1996 to determine if delegates should be elected to a convention to plan the course of sovereignty. Ka Lahui called for a boycott of the election as it was controlled by the state of Hawai'i. Of the over 75,000 ballots mailed out to native Hawaiians throughout the world only 30,000 were returned. Of those who voted, 75% voted to create the convention. The commission has now disbanded and the state says that it will not pay for further elections or a convention. Presently a non-profit group called Ha Hawai'i has been formed to raise the estimated $8 million needed for elections and a convention. In an election staged by Ha Hawai'i on January 17, 1999 to choose delegates to a sovereignty convention less than 9% of Hawaiians who were eligible to vote cast a ballot. Many Hawaiian sovereignty activists boycotted the election. They stated that the whole process was still too closely tied to the state. Ha Hawai'i attributed the poor turnout to a lack of education of the Hawaiian people which led to confusion about the issues involved in the election. They have requested $ 1.9 million from the state Office of Hawaiian Affairs to finance the convention and public relations needed to get the word out to the Hawaiian people. It is their feeling that once the convention gets underway it will arouse the interest of all Hawaiians and people will begin to become more involved in the whole process. The Office of Hawaiian Affairs has countered that the low voter turnout is evidence that a convention is premature at this time.

A very different election is being called for by the sovereignty group called Kanoa, to elect the rightful government of Hawai'i. They feel that the "Bayonet Constitution" that was forced upon King Kalākaua in 1887 is the rightful constitution of the Islands since the government of the United States has already admitted the 1893 revolution was not lawful in Public Law 103-150 which passed in 1993. The group is calling for the election of 24 members to the House of Nobles, and the election of a king or queen to head the government. Their plan would allow non-native Hawaiians to vote in the election as long as they pledge their allegiance to this "lawful government" of Hawai'i.

One of the major points of disagreement between the various groups working for Hawaiian sovereignty is the form that sovereignty should take if it is in fact enacted. There are three forms that could be taken and an infinite number of variables that could be implemented within any one of the three.

The first form would be modeled on the system most common in tribes of Native Americans. Sovereignty is limited to specific areas with the federal government maintaining ultimate control. Almost all of these treaties were established over 100 years ago. With the present legal resources available to them native Hawaiians could undoubtedly draft an agreement that would be more favorable to their interests than the treaties drafted during the 1800's and earlier by native tribes in the continental U.S.

The second option is quite a bit more complicated. Under this form native Hawaiians would be granted autonomous units within the state of Hawai'i. These units would be self governing including the right of taxation. This would provide the revenue source to establish successful communities without the need for government handouts and the strings which typically accompany them. Present lands controlled by the OHA would be the obvious starting point to decide where these units might be located. The island of Kaho'olawe would be another source of land for Hawaiian occupation, once all of the unexploded ordinance is removed from this former Naval bombing range. How these units would interact with the state and federal government would require a lot of detailed negotiations. Ka Lahui has estimated that between Hawaiian Homelands and Crown Lands, that were taken by the U.S. at annexation, almost one and three-quarter million acres should be available.

The third, and most intimidating of the options for non-natives, is complete independence from the United States. While some dismiss this option as unattainable, it would not necessarily be as catastrophic a change as one might imagine. The U.S. Navy could still lease Pearl Harbor as they did in the time before territorial status. The tourist infrastructure would not be dismantled as the new government would recognize this major source of income. In the age of expanding democracy it is unlikely that the islands would return to a traditional monarchy. Issues such as who would be eligible for citizenship would warrant careful examination. There is no reason to assume that total independence would result in the creation of a system that would be unpalatable to all non-native Hawaiians.

The process of attaining sovereignty is a slow one. All of the groups have made their proposals in intentionally vague terms so, regardless of which system is chosen, there will still be plenty of room for compromise. Whatever form sovereignty may finally take, there are still a multitude of decisions to be made. At some point these proposals will need to be examined by the federal and state governments, and all current residents of the islands who are not native Hawaiians. This will begin a process of negotiation that, hopefully, will not lead to violence against person or property. Good faith and patience are attributes that will be required of all for a satisfactory resolution to issues unresolved since 1893.

These are exciting times in Hawai'i. The issue of environmental protection vs. development is nowhere more critical than in Hawai'i. But the fact that development is contingent on peoples' fantasies of a tropical paradise means that environmental concerns can't be ignored. Diversification of the economy is a topic that is widely debated everywhere in the islands. While transportation costs rule against traditional manufacturing, the high tech revolution has the potential of creating a large number of high paying jobs in the software industry. These jobs require an excellent system of public education and better schools would be advantageous for everyone. In the words of Mark Twain, the promise of the new millennium can be realized in "the loveliest fleet of islands that lies anchored in any ocean".

For further reading . . .

Beckwith, Martha. *Hawaiian Mythology*. Honolulu:
University of Hawai'i Press. 1970

Coffman, Tom. *Catch a Wave; A case study of Hawaii's new politics*. Honolulu:
University of Hawai'i Press. 1970

Crawford, Peter. *Nomads of the Wind*. London: BBC Books. 1993

Daws, Gavin. *Shoal of Time : A History of the Hawaiian Islands*.
Honolulu: University of Hawai'i Press. 1974

Day, A.Grove. *Hawai'i and its People*. Honolulu:
Mutual Publishing. 1955

Dudley, Michael Kioni and Agard, Keoni Kealoha. *A Call
for Hawaiian Sovereignty* . Honolulu:
Na Kane O Ka Malo Press. 1990

Fuchs, Lawrence H. *Hawai'i Pono: A Social History*.
New York: Harcourt, Brace, and World.1961

Joesting, Edward. *Hawaii, An Uncommon History*.
New York: W.W.Norton. 1972

Kent, Noel J. *Hawai'i Islands Under the Influence*.
New York and London: Monthly Review Press. 1983

Liliuokalani, Queen. *Hawai'i's Story by Hawai'i's Queen*.
Boston: Lee and Shepard. 1898

Mitchell, Donald D.Kilolani. *Resource Units in Hawaiian
Culture*. Honolulu: The Kamehameha Schools Press. 1982

Morgan, Joseph R. *Hawai'i A Unique Geography*.
Honolulu: Bess Press. 1996

Nordyke, Eleanor C. *The Peopling of Hawaii*. Honolulu:
East-West Center, Univerity of Hawai'i Press. 1977

Oliver, Anthony M. *Hawai'i Fact and Reference Book*.
Honolulu: Mutual Publishing. 1995

Wright, Theon. *The Disenchanted Isles*. New York:. The Dial Press. 1972

Glossary

ahi - yellow fin tuna

aina - land

ahupua'a - system of land division that includes land from the coast to the mountains

akua - lesser gods

ali'i - royalty in the monarchy system

ali'i nui - prime minister

aloha - greeting, love, sharing

au - blue marlin

'aumākua - ancestral spirits

grinds - food

hala - pandanus tree

hale - house or home

hanai - adopted child

haole - foreigner, white person

hapa - one-half, person of mixed blood

Hawai'i nei - all of the islands

heiau - ancient Hawaiian temple

hui - group, syndicate

hula - dance, used in oral history

'ili - land section within ahupua'a

imu - underground oven for slow cooking

issei - first generation Japanese

kahili - feathered staff of ali'i

kahuna - knowledgeable one, priest

kama'aina - long time resident

kanaka - commoner

Kane - chief God, man

kapu - taboo, forbidden, sacred

kapu moe - highest ranking ali'i, prostration taboo

keiki - child, children, young plant

koa - valuable hardwood tree

kokua - help out, cooperation

kona - leeward coast

konane - game like checkers

kuhina nui - prime minister
kuleana - family land holding
kupuna - grandparents or elders
lanai - porch or deck
lei - flower garland
lilikoi - passion fruit
limu - a type of seaweed
Lono - God of the harvest
luau - large feast
luna - overseer on a plantation
mahalo - thank you
maka'āinana - commoners
makahiki - harvest festival
makai - towards the sea
malihini - newcomer
malo - loincloth worn by men
mano - shark
mauka - towards the mountains
mele - song, chant
menehune - little people
nisei - second generation Japanese
ohana - extended family
ono - good, delicious
pake - Hawaiian for Chinese
pali - cliff
paniolo - cowboy
pau hana - finished with work
Pele - Goddess of volcanoes
poi - food staple made from taro
pono - good, righteous
sansei - third generation Japanese
tapa - cloth made from paper mulberry bark
taro - root crop grown in irrigated fields
ti - plant whose leaves are used in cooking
tutu - older woman, grandmother
ukulele - musical instrument with four strings
wahine - woman
wiki wiki - fast, quickly

Index